Spring Floral Necklace

Spring Floral

continued from pages 6 and 7

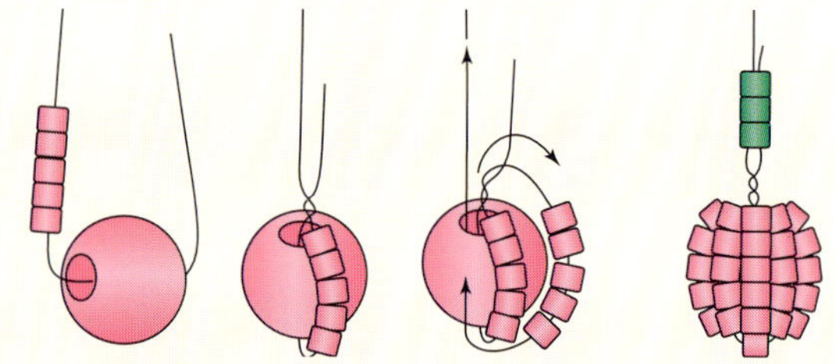

'Berry' - Wrap an E-bead (6° Bead) with Size 14° Beads
Make 'Berries' in Pink and Yellow

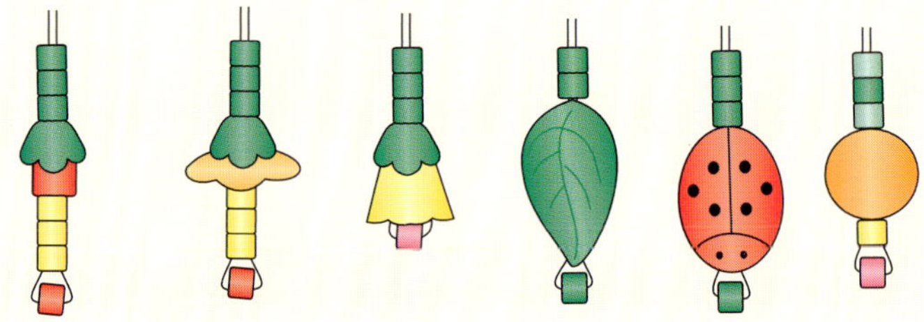

Techniques for Flowers

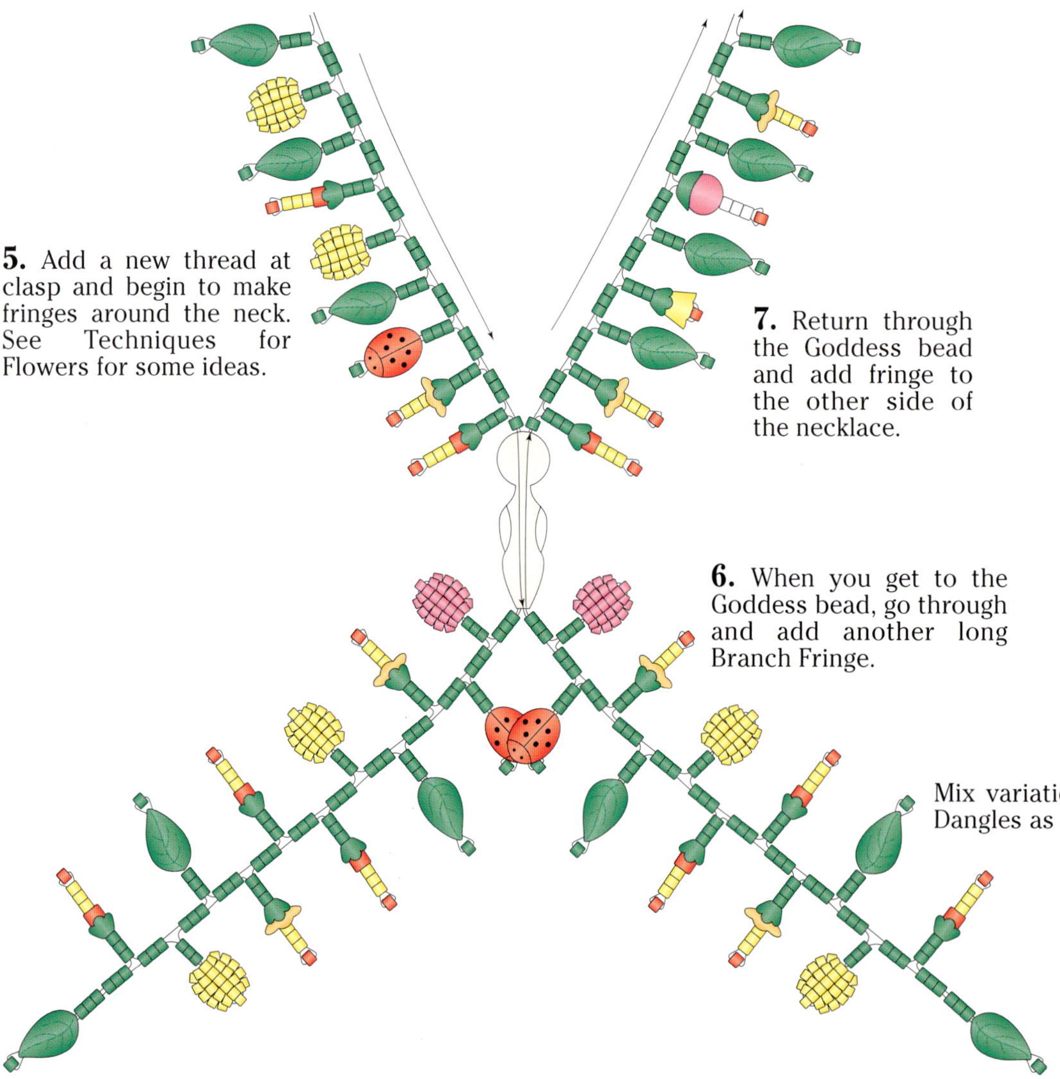

5. Add a new thread at clasp and begin to make fringes around the neck. See Techniques for Flowers for some ideas.

7. Return through the Goddess bead and add fringe to the other side of the necklace.

6. When you get to the Goddess bead, go through and add another long Branch Fringe.

Mix variations of Bead Dangles as desired.

Index of Projects

Flat Peyote - Even Count

If you are learning this stitch you may want to make a small practice swatch.

Rows 1 and 2 - String on 10 beads, using a "stop" bead about 8" from the end of the thread. Use a different size or style bead, so you will not confuse it with the others.

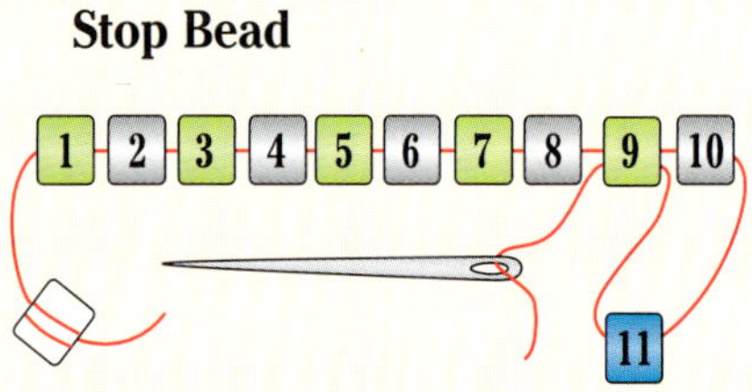

Alternate colors of beads, as shown in the diagram.

You can see on the diagrams that bead #1 would need to be the color of the beads you want in Row 2.

Row 3 - String on bead 11, pass needle through bead 9. (You are "skip-ping" bead 10, the last bead strung.) Continue to add beads 12 - 15.

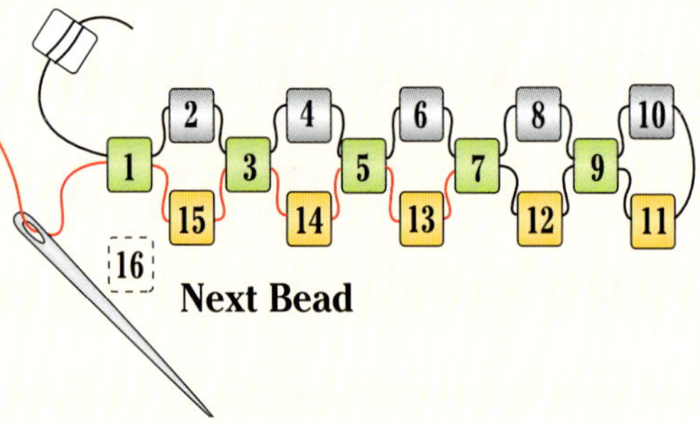

Row 4 - Add bead 16, pass needle through bead 15. Tip: Hold the work carefully at this point, as you do not want the beads to twist out of position. Continue adding beads 17 through 20. Bead 20 is the last bead on Row four.

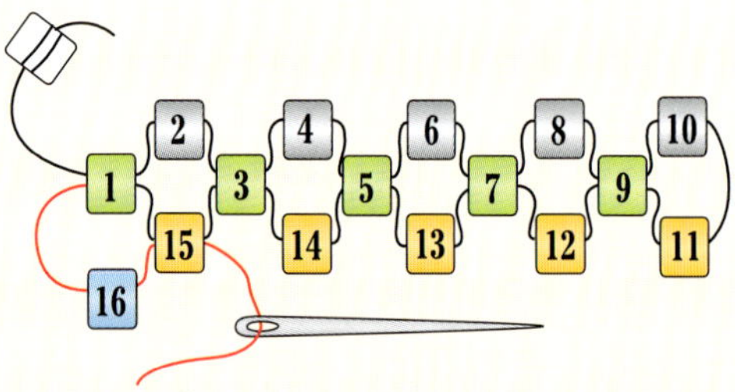

Row 5 - Add bead 21, passing nee-dle through bead 20. Bead 21 is the first bead of row five.

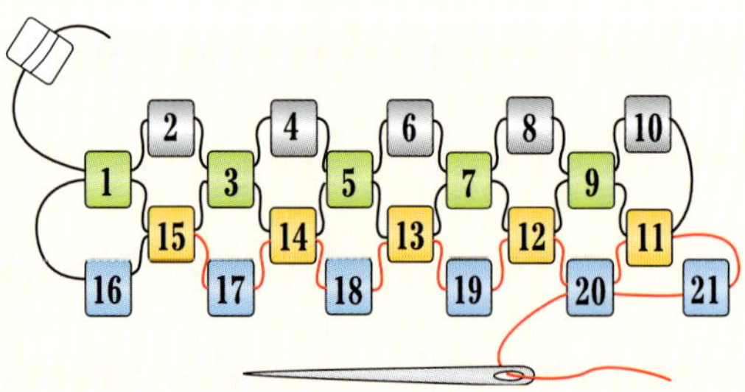

As you add the rest of the beads on row four, you will begin to see how the rows line up with each other, and how the beads fit into each other, like a zipper's teeth.

You will have "down" beads that you go into when adding the next row. If you are using cylinder beads, this will be even more apparent.

Flat Peyote - Odd Count

Odd count Flat Peyote is worked just the same as even count, but one edge will be different.

If you are learning this stitch, make a small piece to practice this odd-count edge turn-around.

Rows 1 and 2 - String on 9 beads, using a stop bead and proceed as for Flat Peyote - Even Count through bead 13.

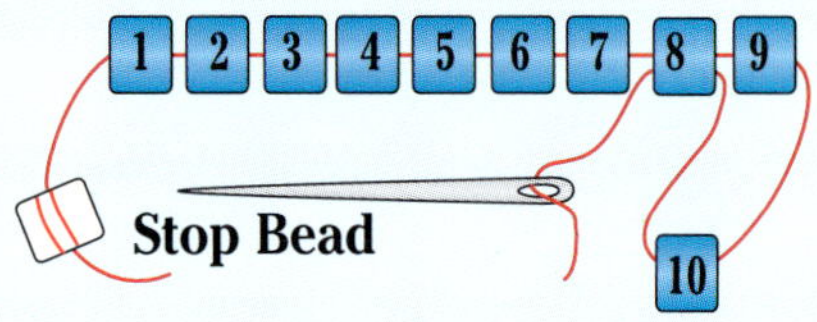

Row 3 - From bead 13 go back through bead 2 and bead 1.

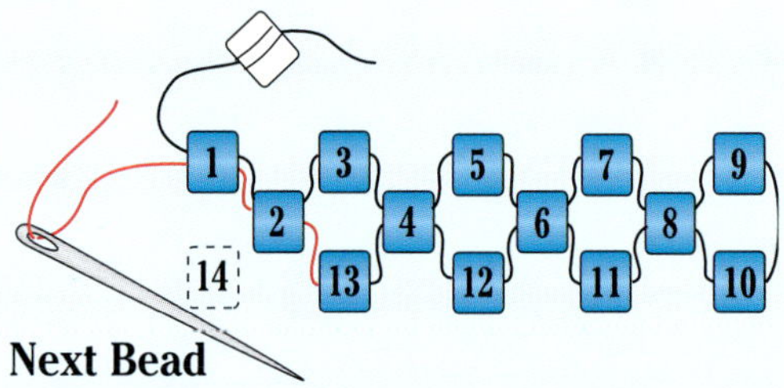

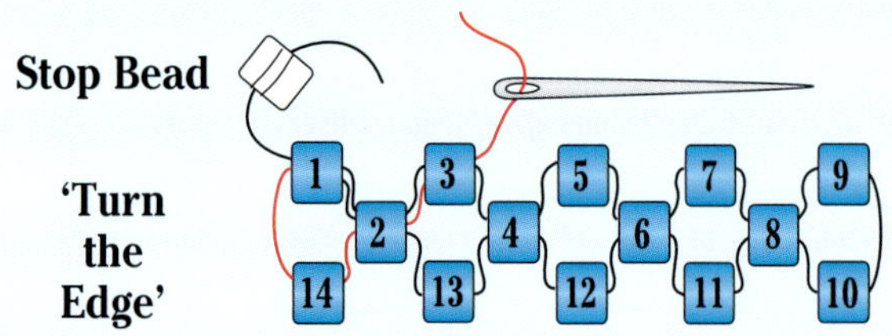

Row 4 - String on bead 14 and go through bead 2 and bead 3, pull beads into place.

Row 5 - Go through beads 13, 2, and 1, and back through bead 14. String on bead 15, go through bead 13 and proceed as usual.

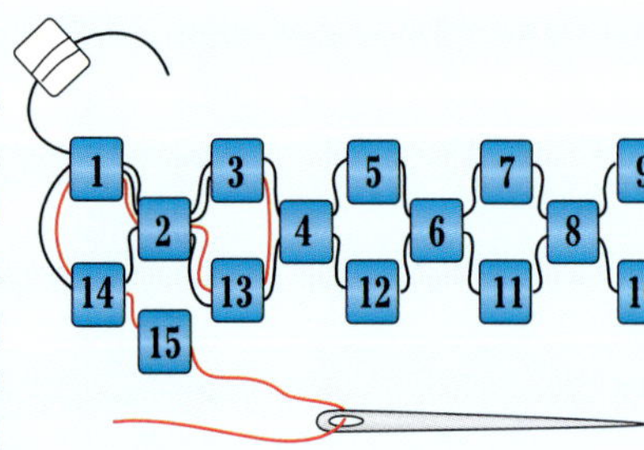

In Flat Peyote - Odd Count, one end will always be done the same way as Flat Peyote - Even Count.

The other end must be 'turned', as in row 3 above, for the first row.

Thereafter, on the odd edge, "loop" around the thread as shown in the diagram.

As an option, you may continue any extra weaving at the odd edge.

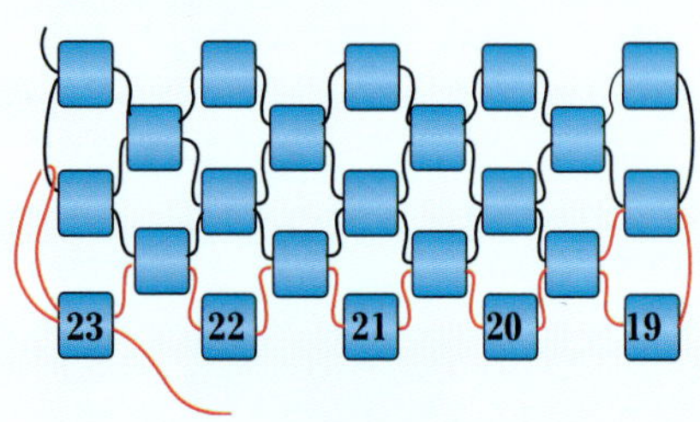

Joining Stitch

Join a seam between two sides of **Flat Peyote** with a 'saw-tooth' or 'zipper' join, take your thread through the first end bead, and through the next bead that fits into the 'zipper' on the other side.

Continue this way, pulling on the thread every 3 or 4 stitches.

Don't pull too tight or your work will warp.

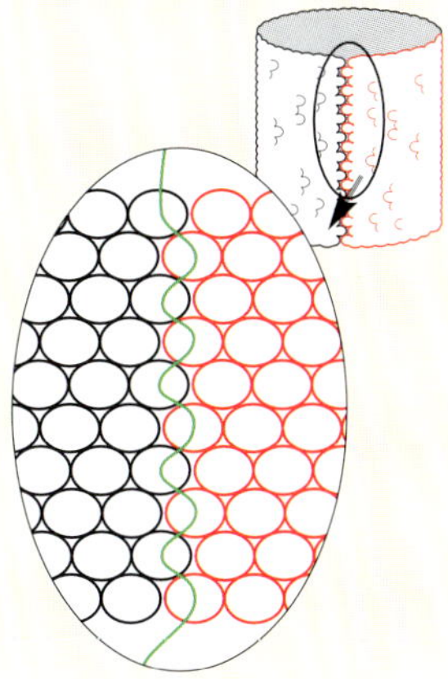

Bottom Fringe

Use illustration as general guide for shaping the skirt front. Your actual bead counts will vary.

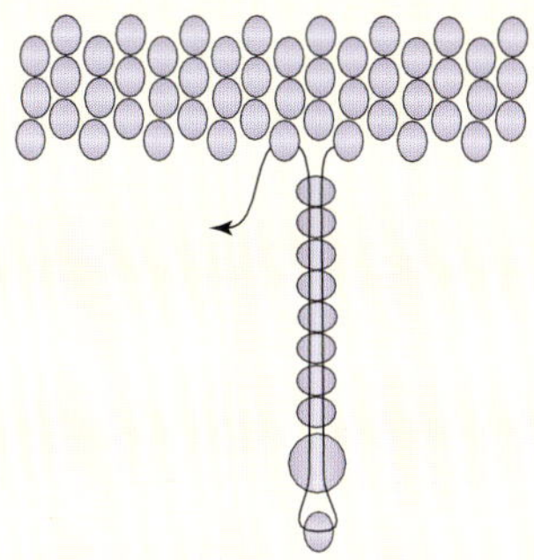

Tubular Peyote

Work as in Flat Peyote.

String on the required number of beads. Tie in a circle, leaving one bead space so the tension will not be too tight as you work the next row.

Step down. Take the needle back through the first bead in the row just completed. You must do this at the end of each row.

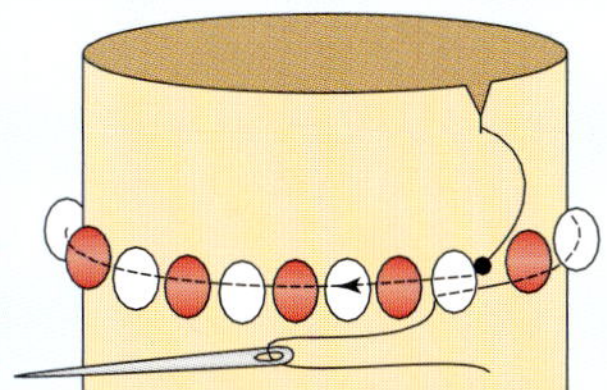

Stepping Down

Take needle back through the 1st bead strung to position thread for the next row.

Work around a center. Use a glass bottle, straw or paper tube.

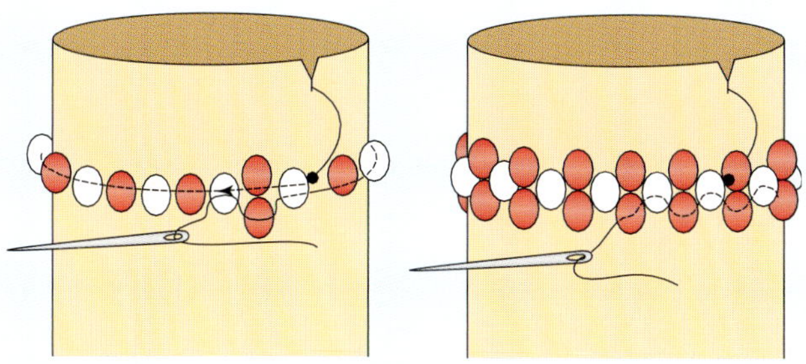

Branch Fringe

Vary the numbers of beads in the beginning strand and on the branches to add variety and interest.

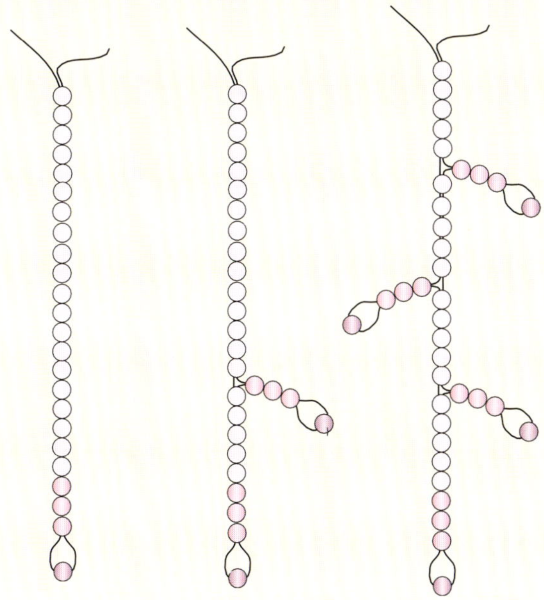

Decrease Beads in a Row

1. Skip one bead on row 1.
2. Add 2 beads in that space on row 2.
3. Add no bead on row 3.
4. Add only 1 bead in that space on row 4.

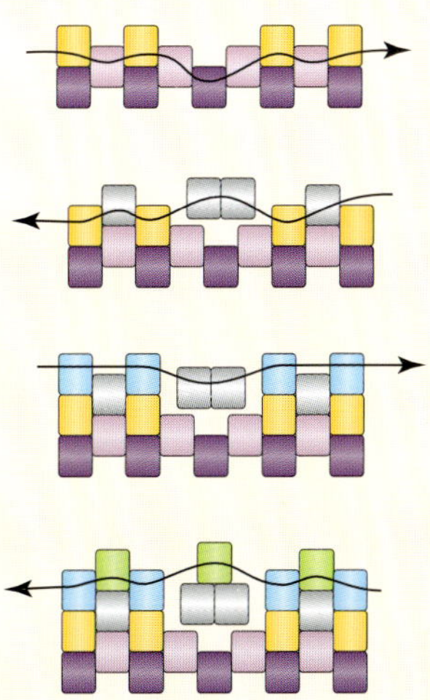

Increase Beads in a Row

1. Bead as usual.
2. On the next row, add 2 beads in one bead space.
3. On the next row, add 1 bead between the two beads.
4. On the next row, add a bead in every space (beads increased to 5).

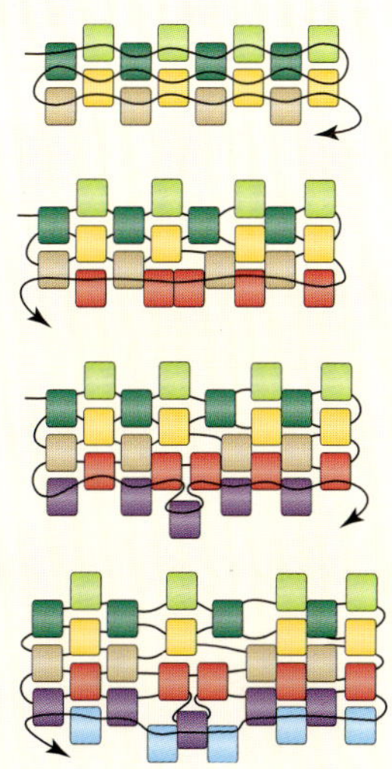

Floral Necklace

beaded by Jill Cremer and Freeway Beaders

SIZE: 28" around

STITCHES:
- Stringing
- Branch Fringe

MATERIALS:

Goddess - 1¾" glass bead

Size 11° seed beads
- Clear Grass Green
- Metallic Green AB
- Silver Lined Fuchsia
- Silver Lined Yellow
- Yellow AB
- White Iris

Size 14° seed beads
- Pink
- Yellow

Assorted fringe beads
- Glass flower
- Glass bud beads
- Leaf
- Ladybug
- Glass bead caps
- Pink fire-polish Crystals

'E' beads - size 6°:
- Pink
- Yellow

Beading supplies:
- size B Nymo thread
- needle

OPTIONAL:
- Soft Flex or Beadalon for necklace

Tip: You may want to string your base necklace on Soft Flex or Beadalon for added strength.

INSTRUCTIONS:

Necklace Base:

Measure enough thread to fit comfortably over your head. Add 12". Add a stopper bead, leaving a 6" tail.

1. String half of your necklace beads and the Goddess bead.
2. As you exit the Goddess bead, make your first branch fringe. See Branch Fringe diagram.
3. Bring needle back through Goddess bead, string second half of necklace beads.
4. Knot the ends of threads and weave ends into beads.

   Or you can add a toggle clasp to make a shorter necklace.

Fringe:

5. Add a new thread at clasp and begin to make fringes around the neck. See fringe diagrams for some ideas.
6. When you get to the Goddess bead, go through and add another long branch fringe.
7. Return through the Goddess bead. Add fringe to the other side of the necklace.

Spring Floral

Beautiful blossoms, leaves, and ladybugs celebrate the awakening of the earth in this absolutely gorgeous Spring floral necklace.

continued on page 8

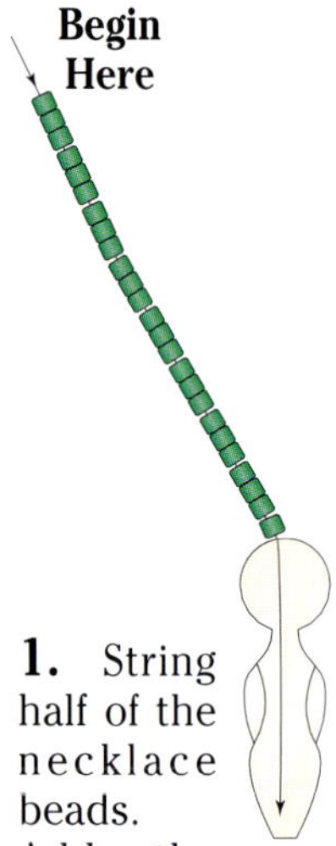

1. String half of the necklace beads. Add the Goddess bead.

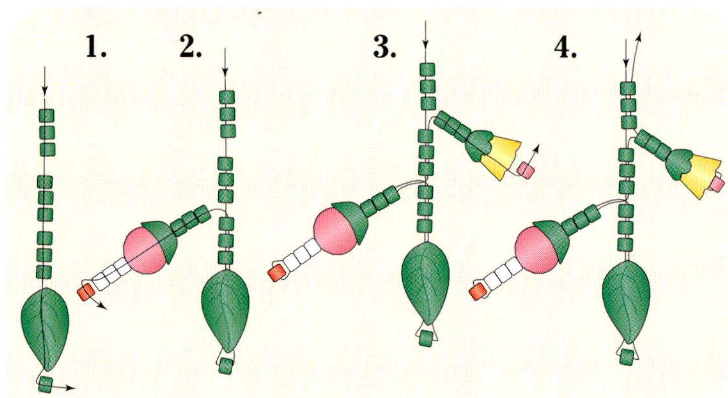

Branch Fringe Diagram

2. As you exit the Goddess bead, make your first Branch Fringe.

See Branch Fringe diagram above and see Techniques for Flowers and 'Berry' on page 8.

4. Knot ends of threads, or add a clasp and weave ends into beads. Or add a toggle clasp to make a shorter necklace.

3. Bring the needle back through the Goddess bead, string the second half of necklace beads.

Friends Earrings

Attach an Earring
Wire at the Top

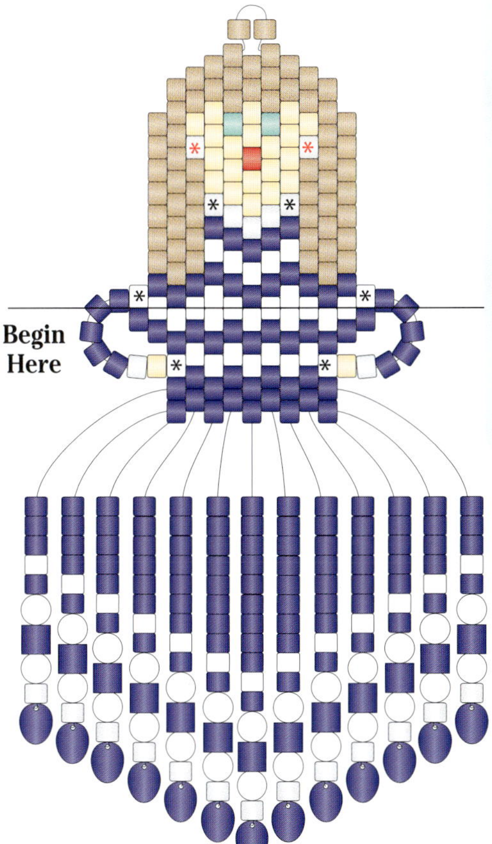

Skirt Fringe
Blue Friend - Make 2

Blue Friend:
Delica beads - size 11°:
- 041 Clear Silver Lined, necklace, bracelet
- 183 Silver Lined Cobalt Blue, dress
- 202 White AB, dress
- 204 Cream Iris, flesh
- 122 Sienna AB, hair
- 704 Clear Red, mouth
- 125 Metallic Green AB, eyes

Assorted fringe beads
- White seed beads

Round beads

Earrings are shown larger than actual size for detail

No outfit is complete without matching earrings. Choose your favorite colors for these dolls.

These small friends are all wearing their own earrings and necklaces. Fabulous fringed skirts complete their outfits.

Attach an Earring
Wire at the Top

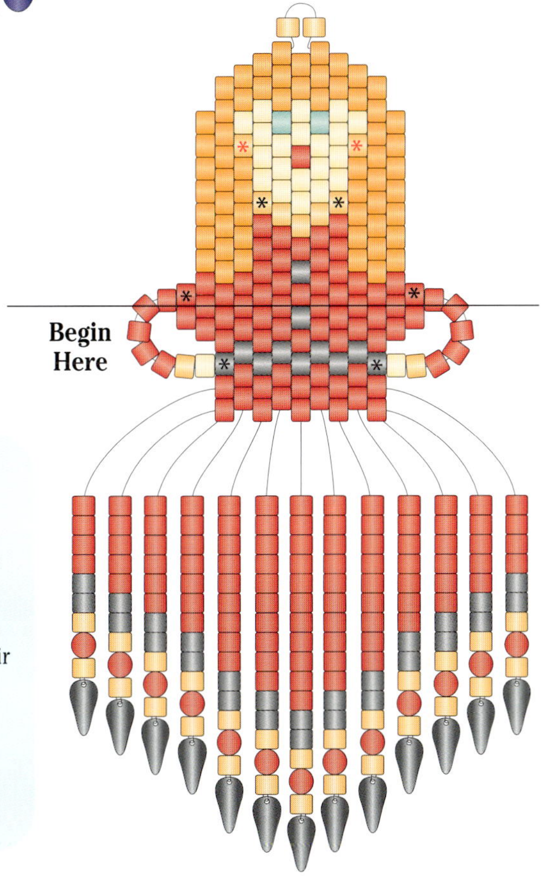

Skirt Fringe
Red Friend - Make 2

* Necklace

* Earring

* Shoulder

* Hip

Red Friend:
Delica beads - size 11°:
- 204 Cream Iris, flesh
- 410 Metallic Gold, face outline
- 704 Clear Red, mouth & dress
- 124 Celery AB, eyes
- 151 Clear Light Orange AB, hair
- 010 Black, buttons & trim

Assorted fringe beads
- Red seed beads
- Dagger beads

Friends Earrings

beaded by Kelly Caleb

STITCHES:
- Flat Peyote - Odd Count, page 4
- Bottom Fringe
- Stringing

SIZE: 2" long

MATERIALS:

Beading supplies:
- needle
- size B Nymo thread
- Earring wires

See individual lists of beads for Red or Blue friend

INSTRUCTIONS:

Body of Earring:
Work down the chart from “Begin Here”. Return to “Begin Here” and work to the top of the chart. Knot thread.

Arms:
Exit thread out the left side of marked shoulder bead. Add 5 beads in dress color, 1 bead in bracelet color, and 1 bead in skin tone.

Enter into the left marked hip bead.

Repeat on the right side of friend.

Embellishments:
Add a necklace and earrings, tacking the center bead of necklaces to blouse. **Skirt Fringe:**
Add fringe to each bead in the last 2 rows of the skirt to form fringe.

Earring:
Add an earring wire with a bead loop at the top.

Circle of Friends Bracelet

Here's a chance to include more of your friends in a "circle of friends" tribute. There is strength in numbers and this tribe of women definitely has power. The band is created with a Flat Peyote stitch, and the fringe skirts are as unique as each friend.

continued on page 12

Circle of Friends Bracelet

beaded by Kelly Caleb

STITCHES:
Flat Peyote - Even Count on page 4
Bottom Fringe
Stringing

SIZE: 6½" long

MATERIALS:
1" Silver slide clasp
Assorted accent beads
for necklace, earrings, fringe :
Dagger beads, Seed beads
Bugle beads, or Round beads

Beading supplies:
needle, size B Nymo thread

For ALL Ladies
Delica beads - size 11°:
704 Red, mouth
041 Clear Silver Lined, Background

INSTRUCTIONS:

Bracelet:

The pattern section is 5" long.

To make the bracelet fit your wrist, add a few rows of beads at the ends.

Weave the entire bracelet with Flat Peyote - Even Count using Delica beads. Add the bracelet band to the slide ends, see page 12.

Arms:

After completing the band, add arms to each friend. Look for the * at each shoulder and hip on the chart. Beginning at the first friend, exit thread out the left side of the marked shoulder bead. Add 5 beads in dress color, 1 bead in bracelet color, and 1 bead in skin tone. Enter into the left marked hip bead.

Repeat on right side of friend.

Move to the next friend, exit thread out the left side of the marked shoulder bead, add 5 beads in dress color, 1 bead in bracelet color, and 1 skin tone bead.

Now bring your needle over and through the arm of the first friend. Arms will be interlocked. Enter into the left marked hip bead on second friend.

Continue for each friend in row.

Embellishments:

Create distinct personalities and styles for your friends. Add a necklace and earrings, tacking the center bead of necklaces to each blouse. Add fringe.

Front View of Bracelet

Lady #1
Delica beads - size 11°:
203 Cream Iris, flesh
010 Black, hair
027 Green Topaz, eyes
161 Orange AB, necklace
073 Violet Lined Clear AB, shirt
721 Opaque Yellow, skirt

Lady #2
Delica beads - size 11°:
067 Pale Peach, flesh
054 Apricot Lined AB, hair
183 Silver Lined Cobalt Blue, eyes
031 Metallic Gold, necklace & belt
124 Celery AB, shirt
027 Green Topaz, skirt

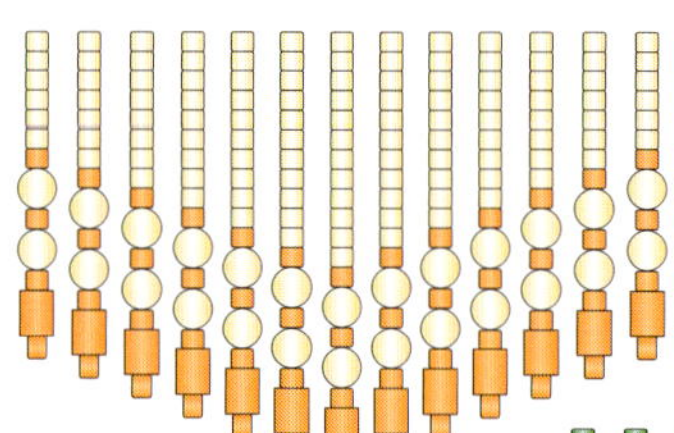

Skirt Fringe:
Add fringe to each bead in the last 2 rows of the skirt.

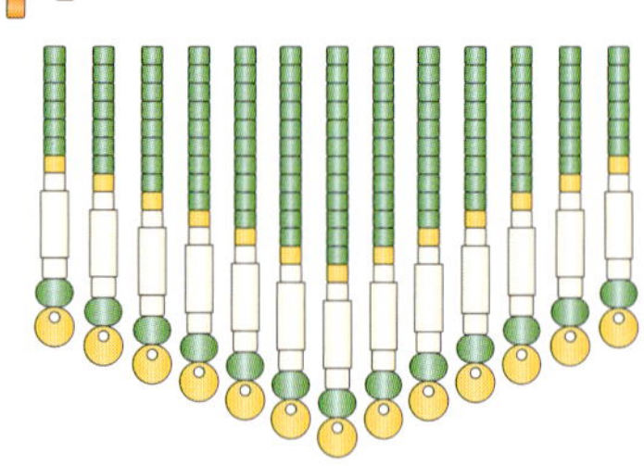

Back View of Bracelet Shows Girls without Earrings, Necklace and Arms

Join Charted Pattern Together Here

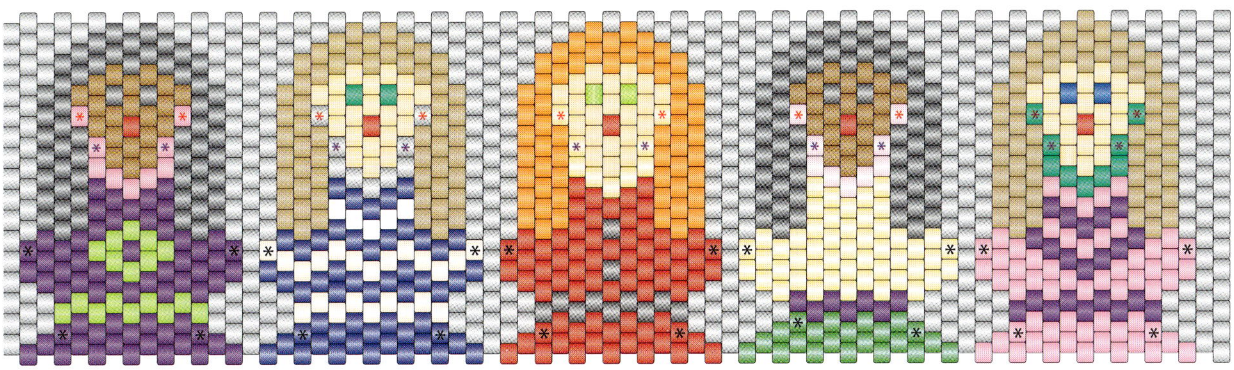

Lady #3

Delica beads - size 11°:

- 653 Brown, flesh
- 010 Black, hair & eyes
- 1345 Silver Lined Dark Fuschia, dress
- 124 Celery AB, designs
- 073 Violet Lined Clear AB, necklace

Lady #4

Delica beads - size 11°:

- 203 Cream Iris, flesh
- 054 Apricot Lined AB, hair
- 027 Green Topaz, eyes
- 041 Clear Silver Lined, necklace
- 202 White AB, dress
- 183 Silver Lined Cobalt Blue, dress

Lady #5

Delica beads - size 11°:

- 203 Cream Iris, flesh
- 151 Clear Light Orange AB, hair
- 124 Celery AB, eyes
- 010 Black, belt
- 704 Clear Red, dress
- 031 Metallic Gold, necklace

Lady #6

Delica beads - size 11°:

- 653 Brown, flesh
- 010 Black, hair & eyes
- 073 Violet Lined Clear AB, necklace
- 721 Opaque Yellow, shirt
- 1345 Silver Lined Dark Fuschia, belt
- 024 Green Amber, skirt

Lady #7

Delica beads - size 11°:

- 203 Cream Iris, flesh
- 054 Apricot Lined AB, hair
- 183 Silver Lined Cobalt Blue, eyes
- 073 Violet Lined Clear AB, dress
- 1345 Silver Lined Dark Fuschia, belt & dress motif

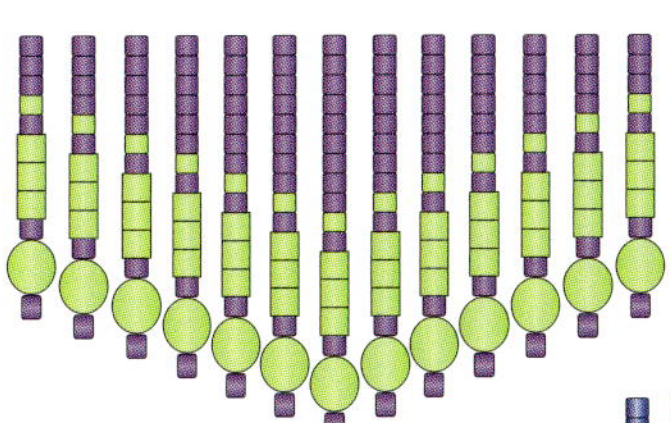

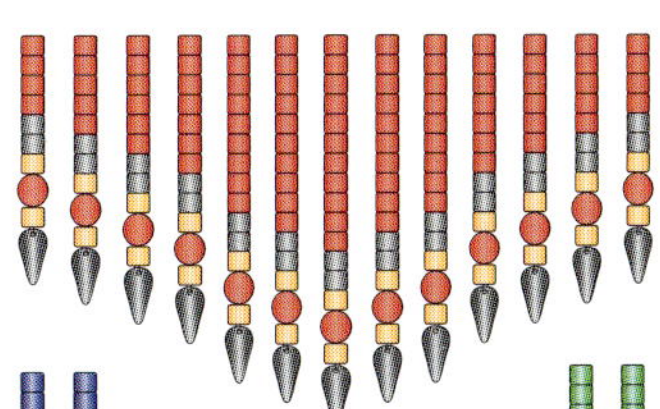

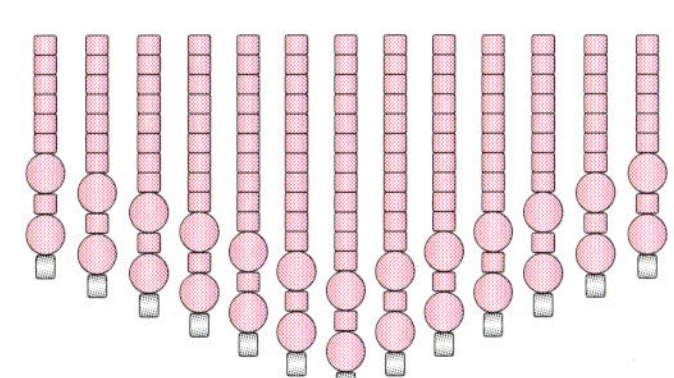

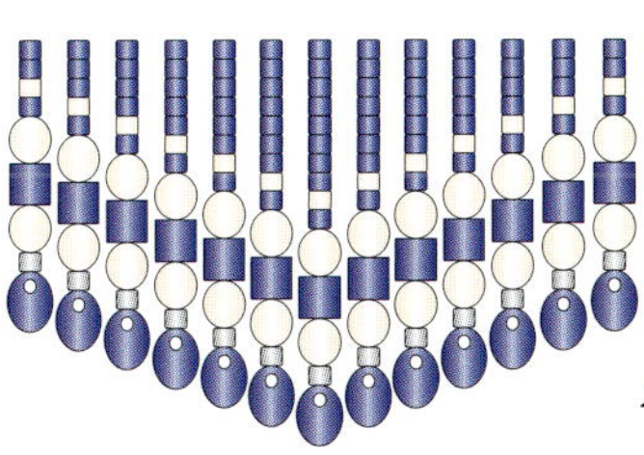

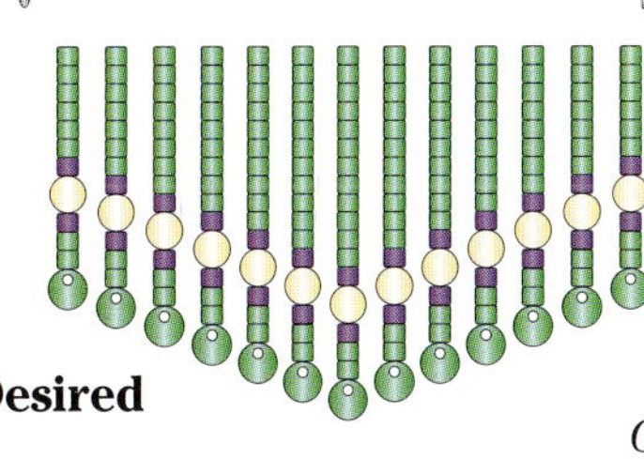

Add Fringe As Desired

Circle of Friends Bracelet

continued from pages 10 and 11

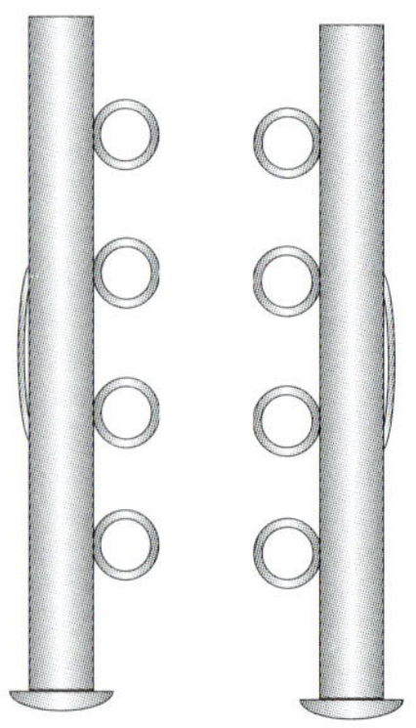

Bracelet Slides

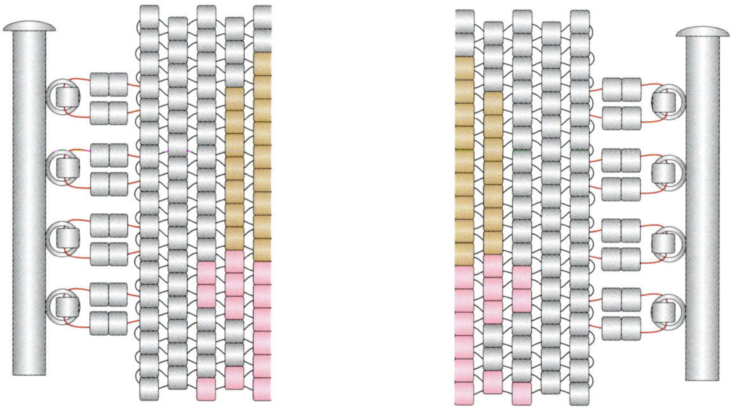

Add a Bracelet Slide to Each End of the Bracelet Band

Circle of Friends Pendant

continued on
pages 14 and 15

Pendant Circle of Friends

Circle of Friends Charted Beading Pattern

This radiant necklace shimmers with beautiful beads that form the images of three friends whose arms are locked in "a circle of friendship".

continued from page 13

Designer's Note:

To begin, think of a couple of individuals who have enriched your life, made you laugh, made you think. They could be your sisters, your children, or your friends. Name their favorite colors and jewelry. List their hair color and skin tones, then choose the colors of beads to use for each little character.

☐ **Omit Bead**

Skip these beads for decrease, add them back for increase.

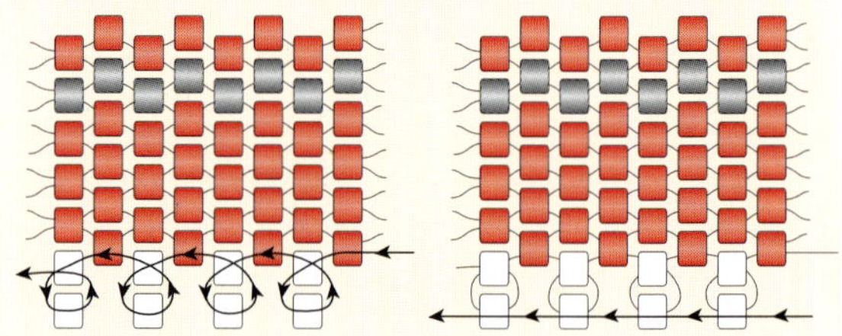

On the last row, decrease around the bottom of bottle by adding one bead beneath each bead.

Run thread through beads, pull up taut and run thread through beads again. Secure thread.

Decrease at the Bottom of Bottle

Circle Of Friends Pendant

STITCHES:
- Tubular Peyote on page 5
- Bottom Fringe
- Stringing

SIZE: 3½" long

PENDANT MATERIALS:
- 25 ml (1¼") clear glass bottle with cork
- 2 Glass donuts 8 mm

Assorted accent beads for fringe:
- Dagger beads
- Seed beads

Beading supplies:
- needle, size B Nymo thread

Cork and Necklace materials:
- Fancy spear head pin 1½" long
- Fancy bead cap
- 30" Soft Flex wire
- Two 2 mm hooks
- 2 crimp beads
- Round-nose pliers

INSTRUCTIONS:

Body of Pendant:

Weave chart in Tubular Peyote with Delica beads. Work down the chart from row marked "Begin Here" to the bottom of bottle.

Decrease beads on the last row on the bottom.

Pull snugly around bottom of bottle. Run thread through the last row of beads again for added strength. Knot.

Return to "Begin Here" line, work to the top of the chart.

See diagrams on pages 4 and 5:
- Decrease beads at the Neck.
- Increase beads at the Neck.
- Decrease at the Top of Bottle.

Pull thread snugly on the last row. Run thread through beads again for added strength. Knot securely.

Delica beads - size 11°:

For All Ladies
- 041 Clear Silver Lined, background
- 704 Clear Red, mouth

Lady #1
- 067 Pale Peach, flesh
- 151 Clear Light Orange AB, hair
- 682 Silver Lined Orange, headband
- 125 Metallic Green AB, eyes
- 031 Metallic Gold, necklace
- 162 Dark Fuchsia AB, dress
- 010 Black, motif

Lady #2
- 340 Matte Copper, flesh
- 010 Black, hair & eyes
- 651 Pale Orange, headband & shirt
- 011 Metallic Olive Green, skirt
- 035 Metallic Silver, belt

Lady #3
- 771 Matte Ecru, flesh
- 054 Apricot Lined AB, hair
- 079 Aqua Lined Clear AB, eyes
- 041 Clear Silver Lined, necklace
- 074 Violet Lined Clear AB, shirt
- 1347 Silver Lined Purple, skirt
- 609 Silver Lined Royal Purple, fringe & belt

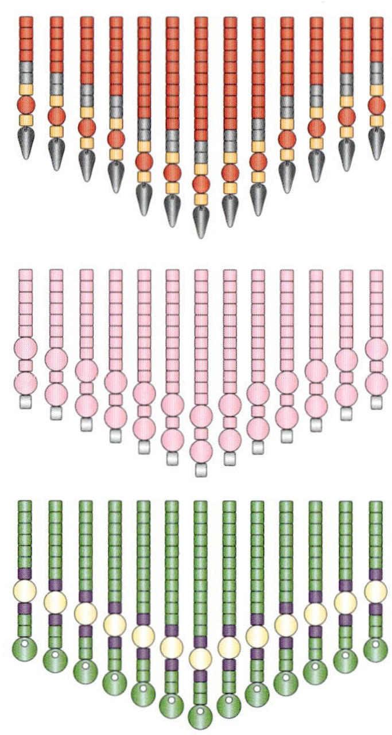

Fringe Patterns

Tubular Peyote

See larger diagrams on page 5.

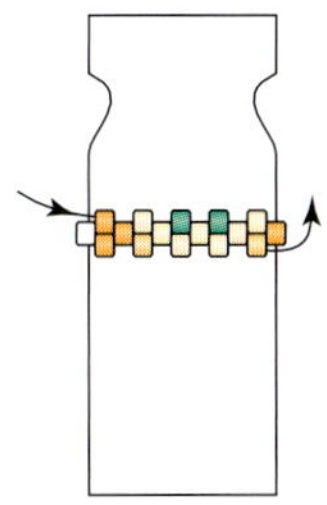

Work Around the Bottle

Tubular Peyote

Actual Size of the Bottle

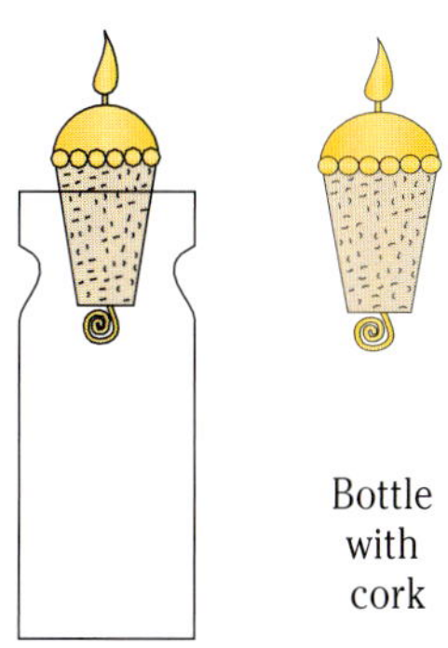

Decorate the Cork in the Bottle

With a needle or long pin, poke a hole through the cork.

Place the fancy bead cap on spear head, put pin through hole.

Secure by curling head pin against bottom of cork with round-nose pliers.

All Three Sides of the Pendant

Arms:

Add Arms to each friend. Looking at chart, you will notice an * at each shoulder and hip. Beginning at one friend, exit thread out the left side of marked shoulder bead, add 5 beads in dress color, 1 bead in bracelet color, and 1 bead in skin tone.

Enter into the left marked hip bead.

Repeat on right side of friend. Move to the next friend, exit thread out left side of marked shoulder bead, add 5 beads in dress color, 1 bead in bracelet color, and 1 skin tone bead.

Now bring your beads, needle and thread over and through the arm of the first friend. Arms will be interlocked.

Enter into the left marked hip bead. Make her other arm, using matching dress, bracelet and flesh beads.

The third friend's arms will interlock with the other friends' arms.

Embellishments:

Locate * on chart for placement of necklace and earrings. Add a necklace and earrings to each friend.

Fringe:

Add fringe to each bead in the last 2 rows of the skirt, using beads to match her dress. Add accent beads and charms as desired.

Necklace Attachment:

At the top of bottle, weave a new thread, string 10 seed beads in your background color. Add a glass donut ring, and close ring.

Take thread through ring of beads again for added strength. Knot.

Repeat on the other side of bottle.

Necklace:

Add a crimp bead to one end of Soft Flex. String beads of your choice to make necklace. End with a crimp bead. Add a hook to each end of necklace. Put hooks through the donuts.

Cork:

With a needle, poke a hole through the cork. Place a fancy bead cap on a spear head, put pin through hole.

Secure by curling head pin against bottom of cork with round-nose pliers.

Egyptian Bracelet

Reminiscent of the treasures of ancient Egypt, this exotic bracelet uses turquoise beads and Carnelian stones with a toggle closure. A beautiful cabochon is held in place by Tubular Peyote stitches woven with gold hex beads. You can turn the bracelet over for a different fashion look.

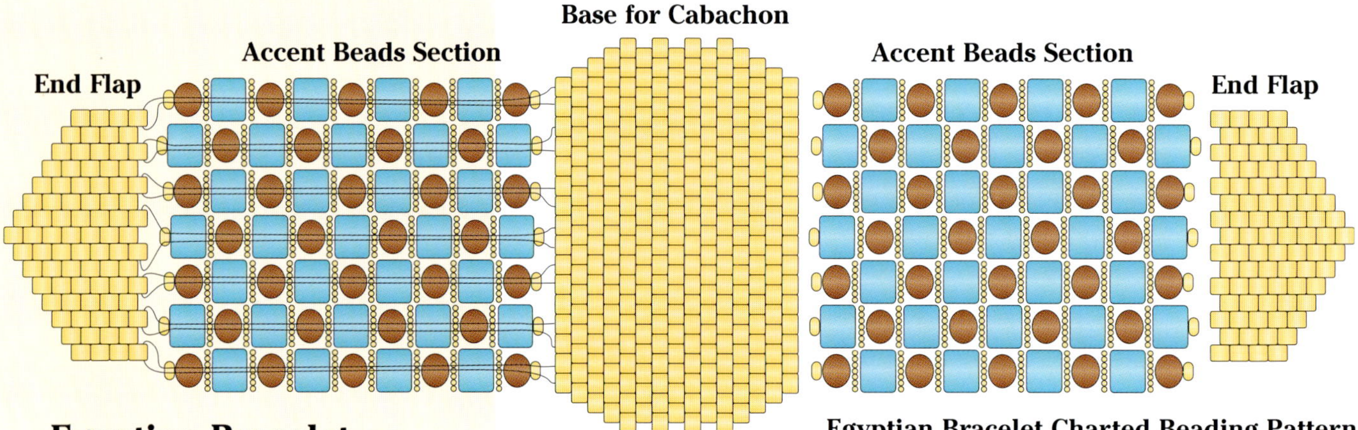

Egyptian Bracelet Charted Beading Pattern

Egyptian Bracelet

STITCHES:
- Flat Peyote - Odd Count on page 4
- Tubular Peyote on page 5
- Stringing

SIZE: 5" long

MATERIALS:
3 x 4 cm cabochon
Assorted beads:
- Size 10° Gold hex beads
- Gold seed beads- size 11°,
- Gold seed beads - size 14°
- 4 mm Carnelian faceted beads
- 6 mm Turquoise rondelles
- 4 mm Gold disk spacer beads

Toggle clasp
Beading supplies:
- needle, size B Nymo thread

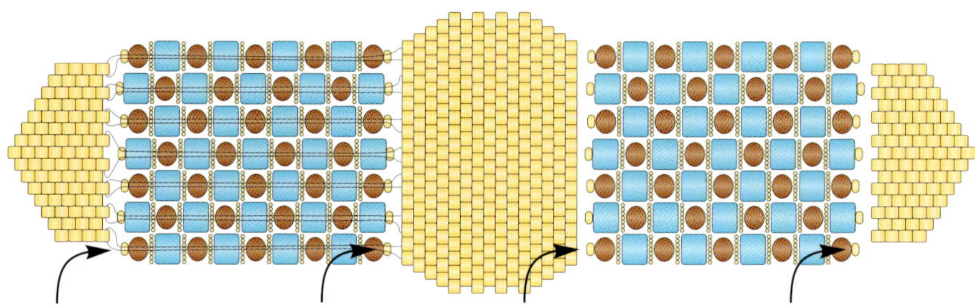

Add Seed Beads to Each End of Bracelet Strands.

Bracelet Front Highlights a Lovely Cabochon Encircled in Gold Beads

Back View of Bracelet

Front View of Bracelet

1. Following the natural curve of your cabochon, weave a Flat Peyote base using Gold hex beads.

2. Center cabochon on base and string enough size 11° seed beads to go around the cabochon.

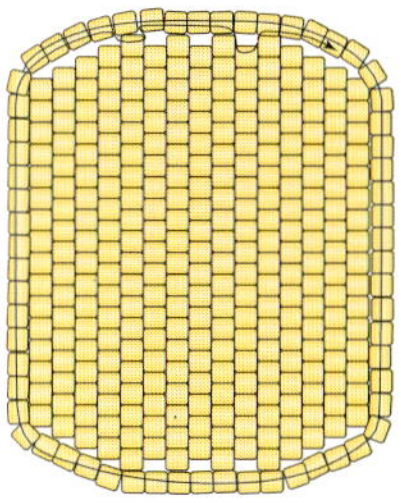

3. Pass needle through first 4 beads in circle. Tack to base all the way around, every 4 - 5 beads.

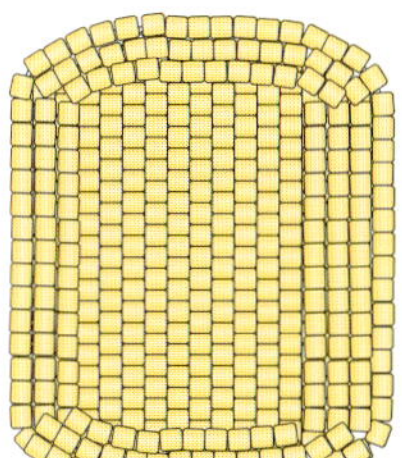

4. Weave 3 - 5 rows of Tubular Peyote, depending on the depth of your cabochon.

5. Place 'cab' in center. Switch to size 14° beads. Weave 2 more rows to secure 'cab' in place.

6. Pull thread taut. Knot securely.

INSTRUCTIONS:

Base for Cabochon:

1. Following the natural curve of your cabochon, weave a Flat Peyote base using Gold hex beads. The base needs to be 3-4 beads wider than the cabochon, and 2-3 beads taller.

Ring Around Cabochon:

2. Secure a thread at one side of base. Center cabochon on base and string enough size 11° seed beads to go around cabochon.
3. Remove cabochon. Make sure you end with an EVEN number of beads, adding a bead if necessary.
4. Pass needle through the first 4 beads in circle. Tack to base. Continue tacking to base all the way around, every 4-5 beads.
5. Weave 3-5 rows of Tubular Peyote (see page 5), depending on the depth of your cabochon.
6. Place cabochon back into center. Switch to size 14° beads. Weave 2 more rows to secure cabochon in place. Add more rows if needed, depending on the particular shape of your cabochon.
7. Pull thread taut. Knot securely.

Bracelet:

Weave both end flaps with Gold hex beads.

Secure a thread to one end flap.

Add an Accent Beads Section to each end flap.

Pass thread through base and back through beads to flap.

Continue to string bracelet portion in this manner until all sections are attached together.

Repeat on other side.

Length of Bracelet:

Measure your wrist. The pattern section is 5" long. Add rows at each end of flaps to fit your wrist.

Clasp:

At apex of triangle flap, add 5 seed beads, string on one end of toggle clasp and secure to apex bead. Take thread through this ring again for added strength.

Repeat on other end of bracelet. You can also use this area to add length by stringing a few accent beads.

Earth Angel Mini Pouch

Luscious deep blue beads play background host to this unusual angel necklace. Like twinkling stars in a night sky, twenty dangles of blue are accented with gold beads.

The back side of the pouch is the same glorious blue with the word 'Angel' woven in gold. The strap contains double rows of blue beads accented with gold and fire red crystals.

Earth Angel Charted Beading Pattern

✱ Place Swags Her

Earth Angel

beaded by Cindy Klein

STITCHES:
- Tubular Peyote
- Flat Peyote - Odd Count, pages 4 - 5
- Bottom Fringe
- Stringing

SIZE: 19" long

MATERIALS:

Beading supplies:
- needle, B Nymo thread

Assorted beads:
- 3 x 5 mm Gold rondelles
- 4 mm Red Crystals

Delica beads - size 11°:
- 771 Matte Ecru, flesh
- 461 Metallic Brown, hair
- 748 Matte Blue, eyes & background
- 704 Clear Red, mouth
- 202 White AB, necklace
- 295 Red Iris, dress
- 160 Yellow AB, dress
- 747 Matte Lt. Blue, dress
- 031 Metallic Gold, wings & letters

Seed Beads - size 11°:
- Yellow
- Transparent Red
- Gold
- Silver Lined Matte Dark Blue

INSTRUCTIONS:

Pouch Body:
Weave the body of the pouch in Tubular Peyote, see page 5.

Paper Tube:

TIP: It is easier to stitch Tubular Peyote around an object than it is to stitch normally. Often you can find a cardboard tube or even a small bottle the correct size to fit inside of the pouch as you stitch.

If you cannot find a cardboard tube the right size, make one from rolled paper, see page 19.

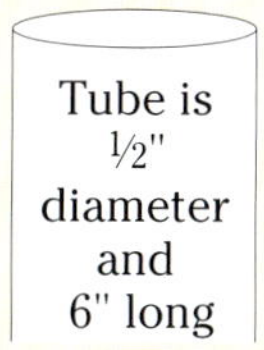

HELPFUL HINT
Roll a piece of stiff paper into a tube ½" in diameter and 6" long. Tape the edge.
Work Tubular Peyote beading around the tube.

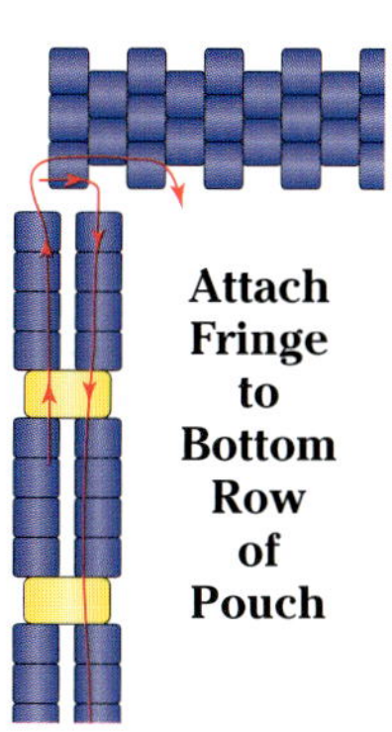

Attach Fringe to Bottom Row of Pouch

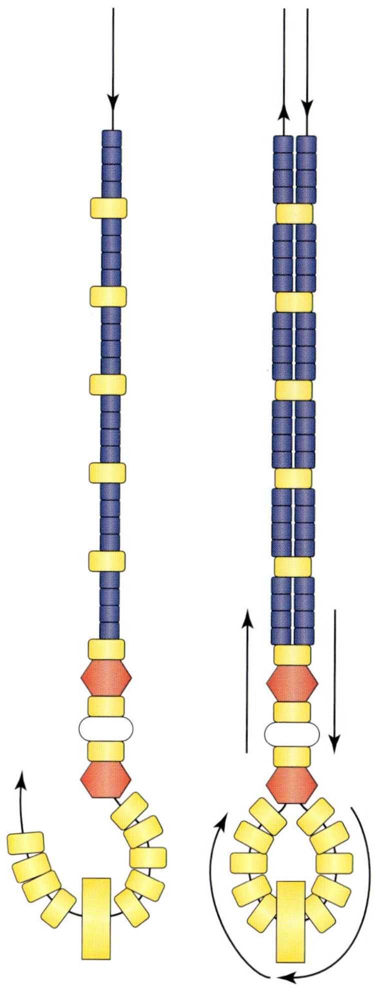

Make 20 Fringes Across the Bottom of the Pouch

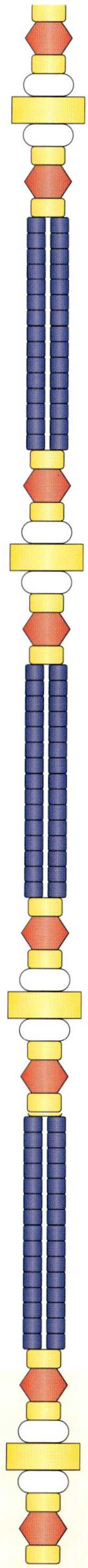

String Beads for Strap Attach Strap

Bottom of Pouch:
Remove the cardboard tube. Weave the flap at the bottom of the pouch.

Close Pouch:
Close the bottom of pouch by stitching beads together.

Fringe:
Add a double row of fringe to the bottom of pouch.

Red Swags:
Attach a thread at an *. String Red beads in a loop then attach at another * (see photo). Repeat to make a second loop.

Necklace Strap:
String beads for the necklace strap until it is the desired length. Attach to pouch on each side as indicated on beading chart.

Ancient Mother

Ancient mother, mother nature, sacred Goddess or just spirit, our figure is the symbol of renewal and regeneration. Depicted here in a lovely pendant, she is honored with fresh water pearls and sparkling crystals.

INSTRUCTIONS:

Pouch Body:
Weave the body of the pouch in Tubular Peyote.

Paper Tube:
TIP: It is easier to stitch Tubular Peyote around an object than it is to stitch normally. Often you can find a cardboard tube or even a small bottle the correct size to fit inside of the pouch as you stitch.

If you cannot find a cardboard tube the right size, make one from rolled paper, see page 21.

Bottom of Pouch:
Remove the cardboard tube. Weave the flap at the bottom of the pouch.

Close Pouch:
Close the bottom of pouch by stitching beads together.

Fringe:
Add a double row of fringe to the bottom of pouch for a really lush look. Each set of fringes is one bead longer toward the center to create graduated length.

Necklace:
String beads for the necklace strap until it is the desired length. Attach to pouch on each side with bead loops and Black glass donuts, as indicated on beading chart.

Back of Pouch

Ancient Mother

STITCHES:
- Tubular Peyote on page 5
- Bottom Fringe
- Stringing

SIZE: 21" long

MATERIALS:

Beading supplies:
- needle, size B Nymo thread

Delica beads - size 11°:
- 310 Matte Black, body
- 295 Red Iris, motif
- 253 Lavender Iris, flower center & eye
- 124 Celery AB, leaf outline
- 031 Metallic Gold, trim & flower outline & inside leaf
- 203 Cream Iris, bag

Seed Beads - size 11°
- Gold
- White

Crystals:
- 3 mm Red bicone
- 4 mm Metallic Gold bicone

Assorted beads:
- 8 mm oval freshwater pearls
- 7 mm Matte Black rice beads
- Two 9 mm Black glass donuts
- Red glass Tanfouk charms
- Gold Goddess charms

2 Silver crimp beads

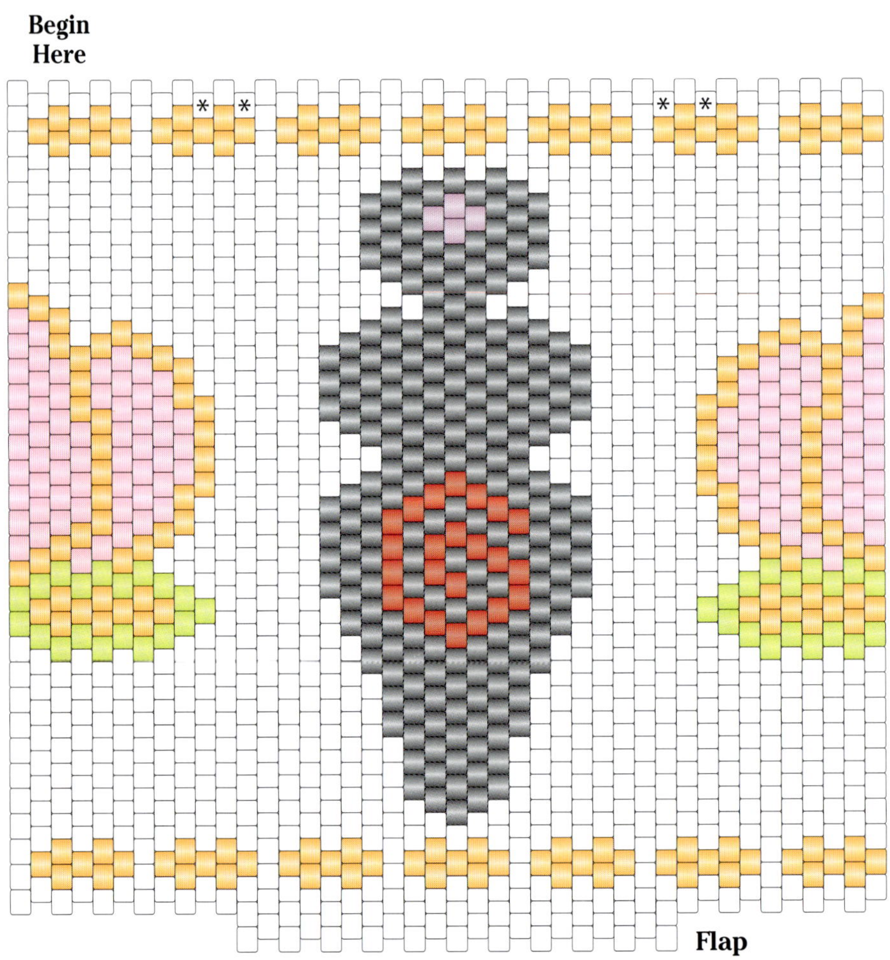

Ancient Mother Charted Beading Pattern

"as a new plant breaks the ground with great difficulty; so must we sometimes push against difficulty in bringing forth our dreams."

from *I Ching* "Chaos"

TIP:
Roll a piece of stiff paper into a tube ½" in diameter and 6" long. Tape the edge.
Work Tubular Peyote beading around the tube.

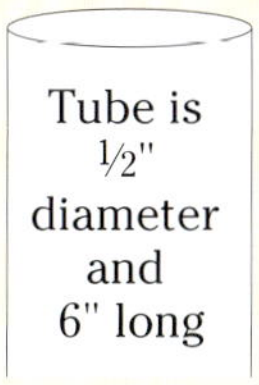

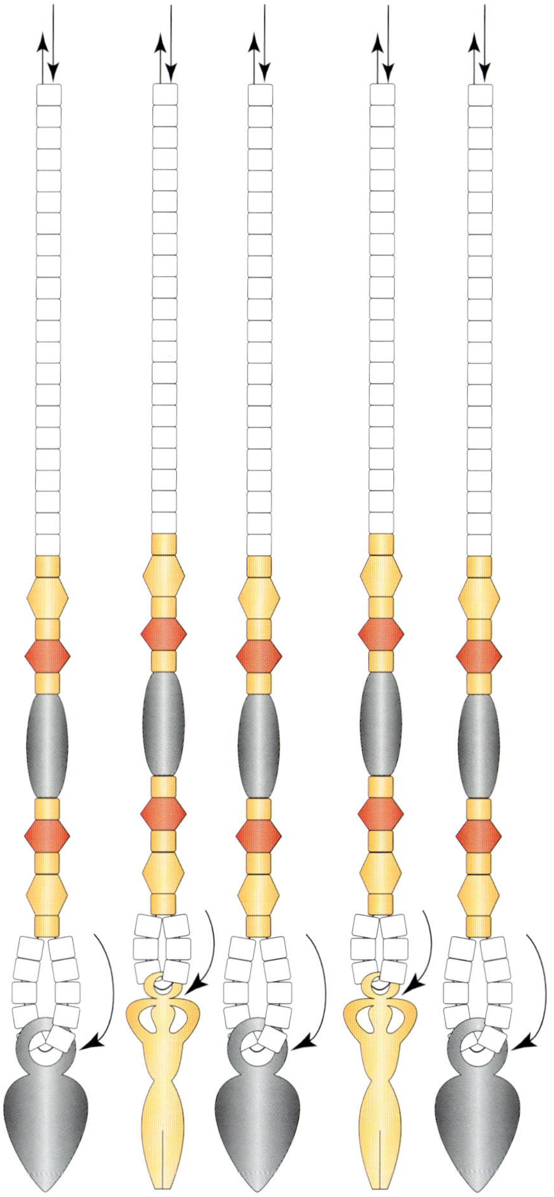

Fringe Patterns
Make 21 Total Fringes

Love Angels Bag

This lovely necklace bag shimmers with red hearts and angels floating in a sky blue background. Angel charms dangle from beautiful fringe, giving blessings in abundance.

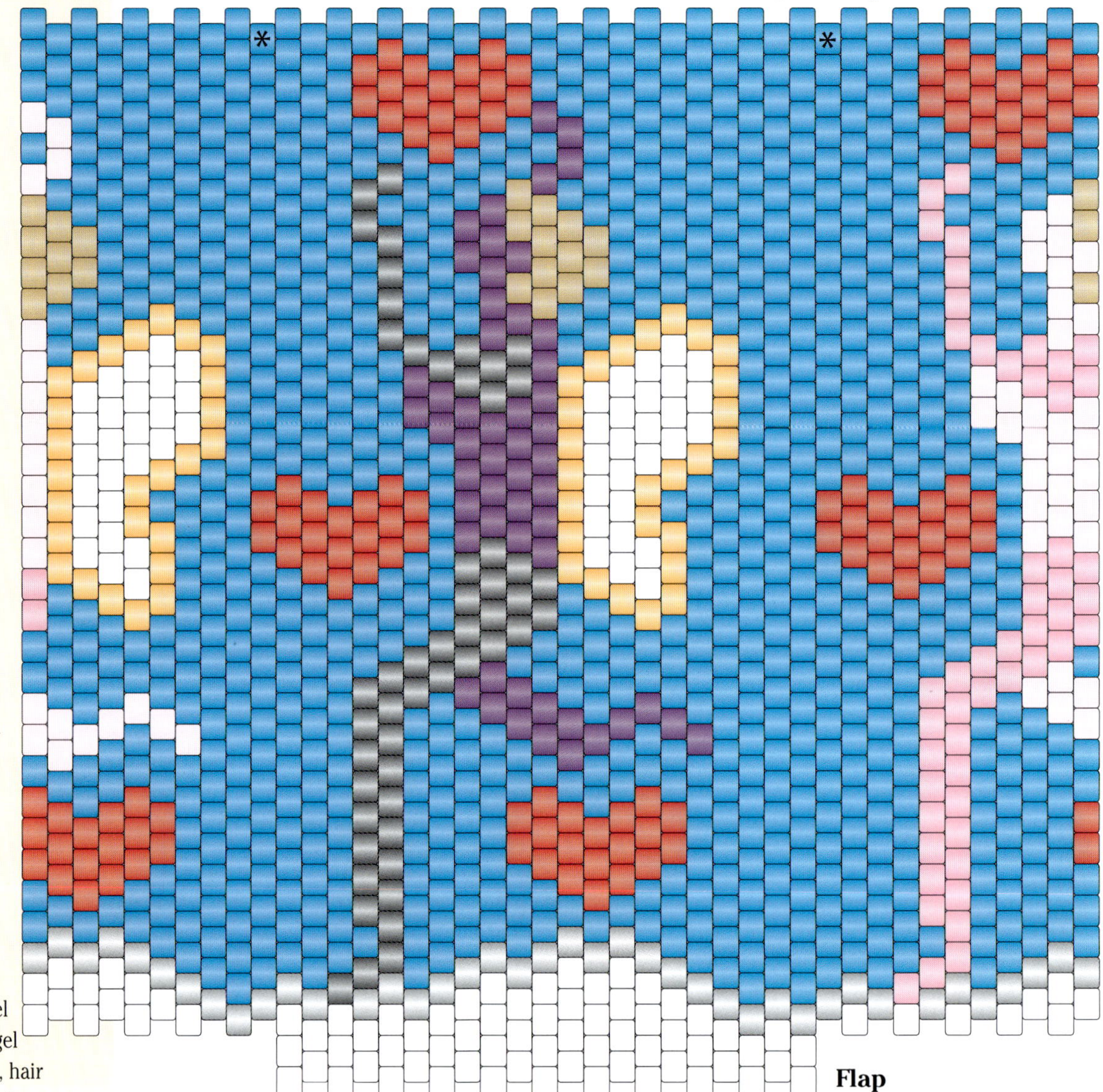

Love Angels Charted Beading Pattern

Love Angels

STITCHES:
- Tubular Peyote on page 5
- Flat Peyote - Odd Count on page 4
- Bottom Fringe
- Stringing

SIZE: 6½" long

MATERIALS:

Beading supplies:
- needle
- size B Nymo thread

Delica beads - size 11°:
- 310 Matte Black, angel
- 001 Shiny Pewter, angel
- 054 Apricot Lined AB, hair
- 202 White AB, inner wings & cloud
- 031 Metallic Gold, wing outline
- 295 Red Iris, hearts
- 085 Blue AB, background
- 041 Clear Silver Lined, cloud
- 208 Tan Iris, flesh, angel
- 204 Cream Iris, flesh, angel

Assorted beads:
- AB Clear Bugle bead
- 6 mm Red glass hearts
- 4 mm Gold disc
- 4 mm Blue Crystal
- 4 mm Clear Crystal bicone
- 3 mm pearls

INSTRUCTIONS:

Bag Body:
Weave the body of the pouch in Tubular Peyote.

Paper Tube:
TIP: It is easier to stitch Tubular Peyote around an object than it is to stitch normally. Often you can find a cardboard tube or even a small bottle the correct size to fit inside of the pouch as you stitch.

If you cannot find a cardboard tube the right size, make one from rolled paper, see page 23.

Bottom of Pouch:
Remove the cardboard tube. Weave the flap at the bottom of the pouch.

Close Pouch:
Close the bottom of pouch by stitching beads together.

Fringe:
Add a double row of fringe to bottom of bag. See diagram.

Strap:
String beads for the necklace strap until it is the desired length. Attach to pouch on each side.

Add Branch Fringes to each side of the strap, see page 23.

TIP:
Roll a piece of stiff paper into a tube 3/8" in diameter and 6" long. Tape the edge.
Work Tubular Peyote beading around the tube.

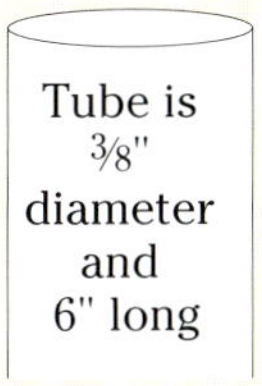

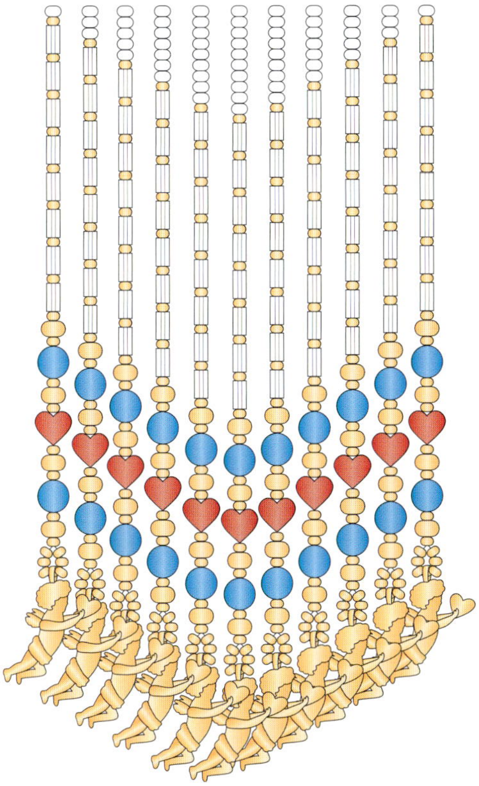

Fringe Pattern
Make 21 Total Fringes

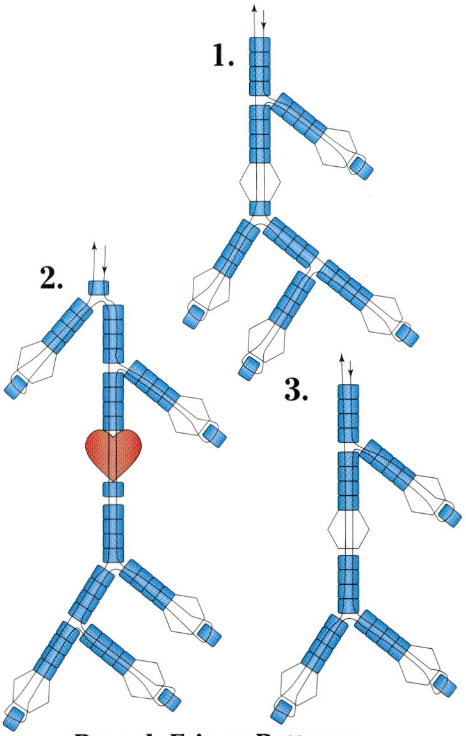

Branch Fringe Patterns
Make 1 Each on Both Sides of Strap

Goddess of the Greatest Gift

A mother's love is like no other. Celebrate a new baby with the Goddess of the Greatest Gift love pouch. This bag is a terrific place to keep the baby's photo handy. This lovely necklace has Goddess images on both sides but in different colors!

continued on pages 26 and 27

Strap Placement *

Begin Here

Flap

Goddess Charted Beading Pattern

Goddess of the Greatest Gift

STITCHES:
- Tubular Peyote on page 5
- Bottom Fringe
- Stringing

SIZE: 23" long

MATERIALS:

Beading supplies:
- needle
- size B Nymo thread

Delica beads - size 11°:
- 310 Matte Black, lady body
- 295 Red Iris, ladies motif
- 001 Shiny Pewter, baby body
- 652 Gray, baby head
- 031 Metallic Gold, motif
- 415 Lt Green, leaf
- 607 Silver Lined Blue Spruce, leaf
- 203 Cream Iris, background
- 371 Fatigue Green, lady body
- 022 Metallic Mahogany, baby body
- 064 Oyster AB, baby head

Assorted beads:
- Gold drop charms
- Seed pearls
- 5 mm Green glass hearts
- 3 mm Red glass hearts
- 4 mm Gold spacer beads
- Gold spacer disc

INSTRUCTIONS:

Bag Body:
Weave the body of the bag in Tubular Peyote.

Paper Tube:
TIP: It is easier to stitch Tubular Peyote around an object than it is to stitch normally. Often you can find a cardboard tube or even a small bottle the correct size to fit inside of the pouch as you stitch.

If you cannot find a cardboard tube the right size, make one from rolled paper, see page 26.

Bottom of Pouch:
Remove the cardboard tube. Weave the flap at the bottom of the pouch.

Close Pouch:
Close the bottom of pouch by stitching beads together.

Fringe:
Add a double row of fringe to bottom of bag. See diagram.

Strap:
String beads for the necklace strap (see page 26) until it is the desired length. Attach to pouch on each side.

Goddess of the Greatest Gift

Pearls are a symbol of wisdom. They are appropriate for representing a mother's love. It takes a wise and caring person to guide a child safely into adulthood.

continued from pages 24 and 25.

HELPFUL HINT
Roll a piece of stiff paper into a tube 1⅜" in diameter and 6" long. Tape the edge.
Work Tubular Peyote beading around the tube.

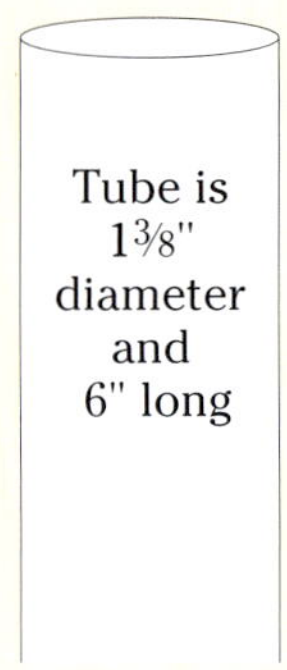

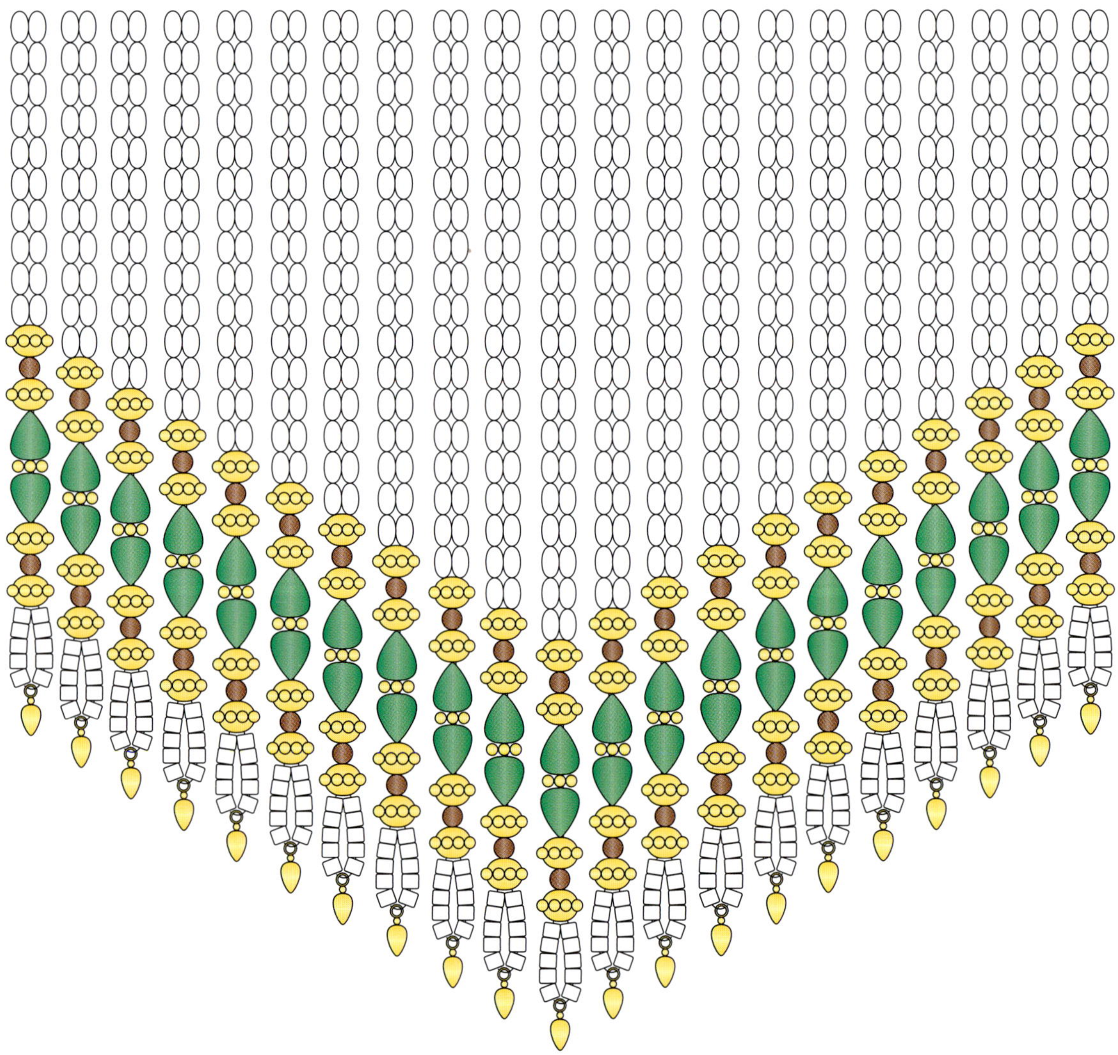

Fringe Pattern

Attach Necklace Strap

Angel of True Love

continued on pages 30 and 31

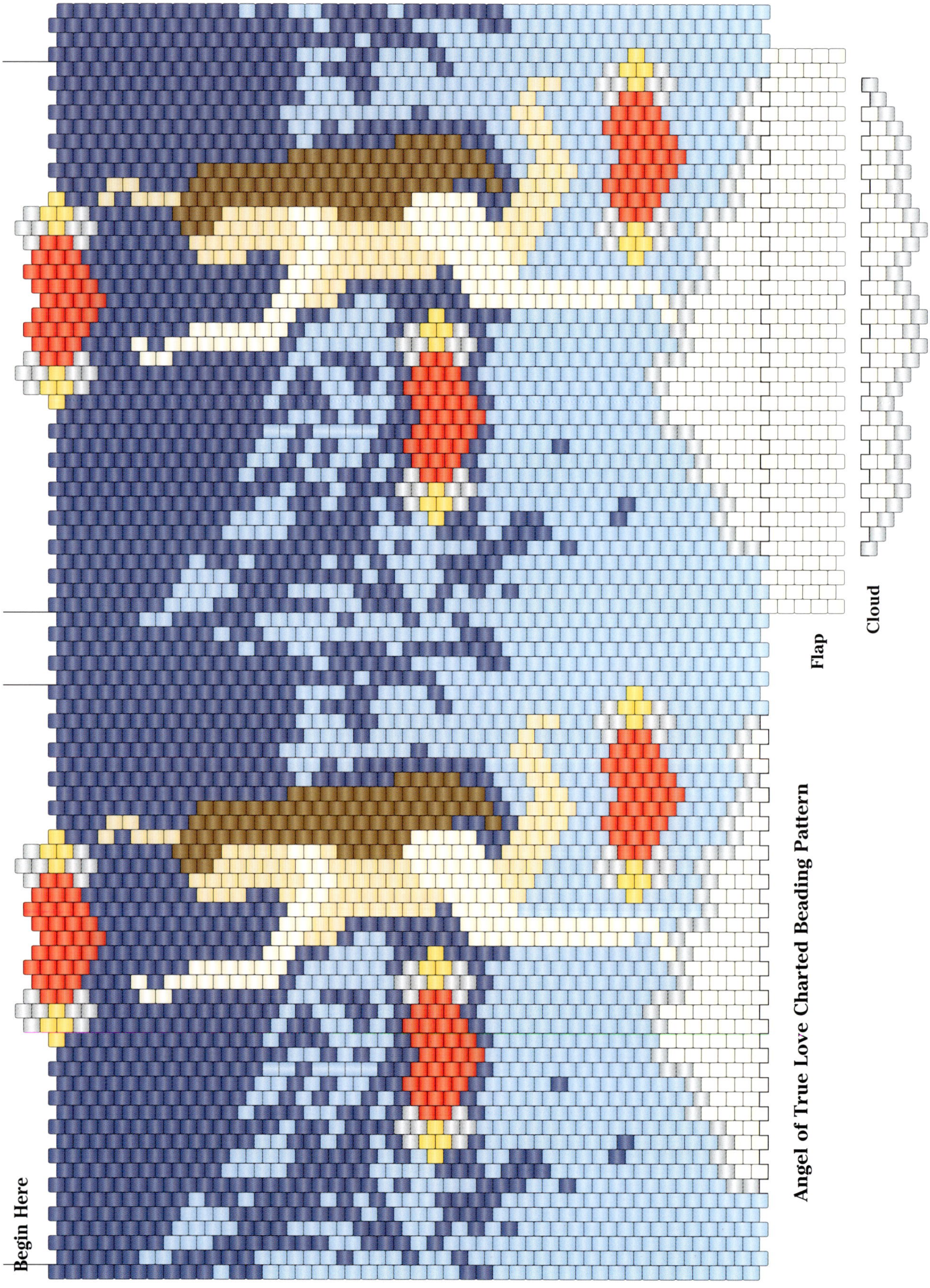

Angel of True Love Charted Beading Pattern

Angel of True Love
Necklace Strap

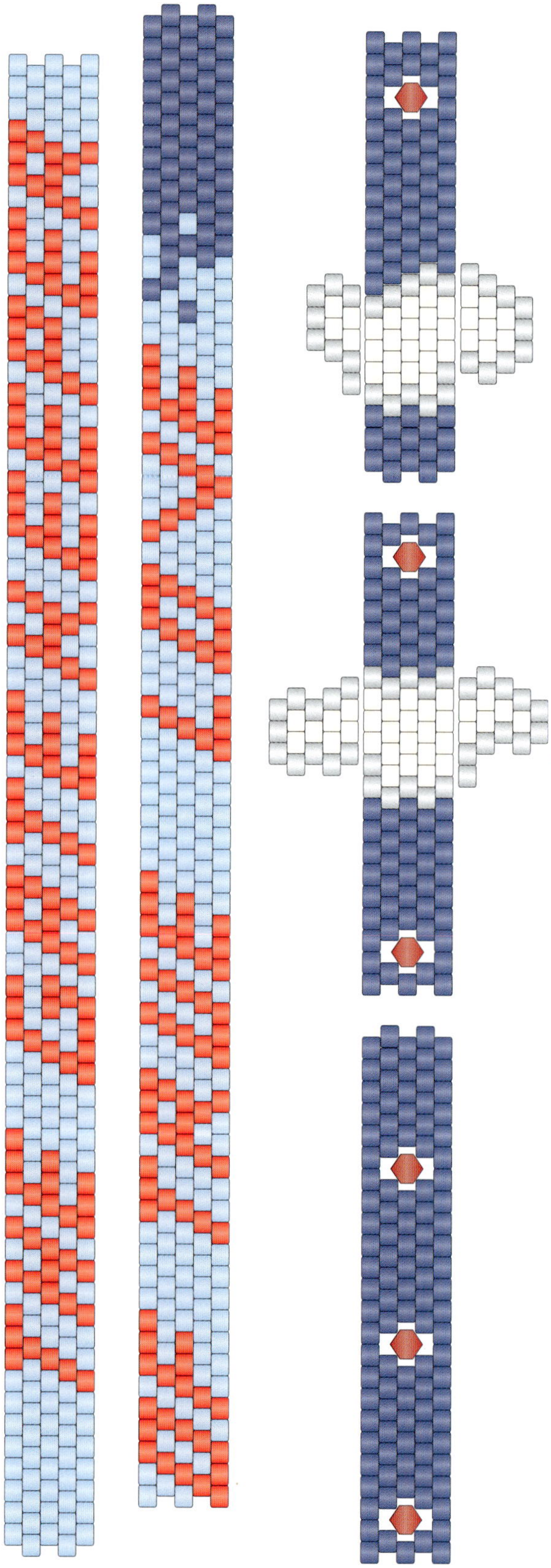

Necklace Strap Charted Beading Pattern

This lovely angel floating on a cloud is the keeper of true love. The necklace is really a pouch where you can carry a photo of your beloved. If you have no true love at present, carry a note with what you would wish him to be. Be very specific. Wishes come true every day.

continued from pages 28 and 29

Make this perfect beaded neck strap for your Angel pouch.

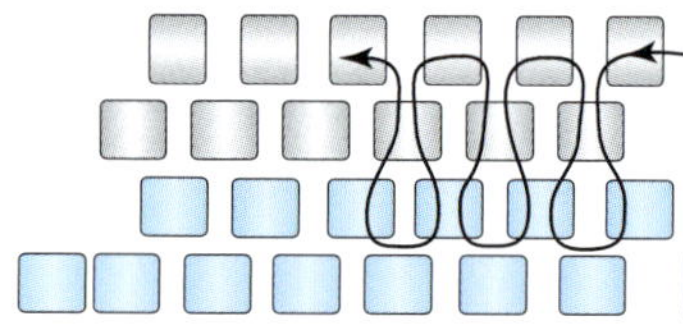

Picot Edge
for Necklace Strap

TIP:
Roll a piece of stiff paper into a tube 1⅜" in diameter and 6" long. Tape the edge.
Work Tubular Peyote beading around the tube.

String Graduated Lengths of Fringe.

Center of the Pouch:

56 light blue beads
56 dark blue beads

Edges of the Pouch:

40 light blue beads
40 dark blue beads

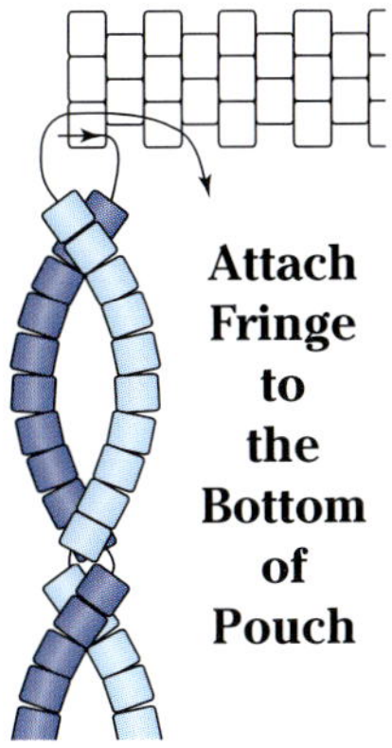

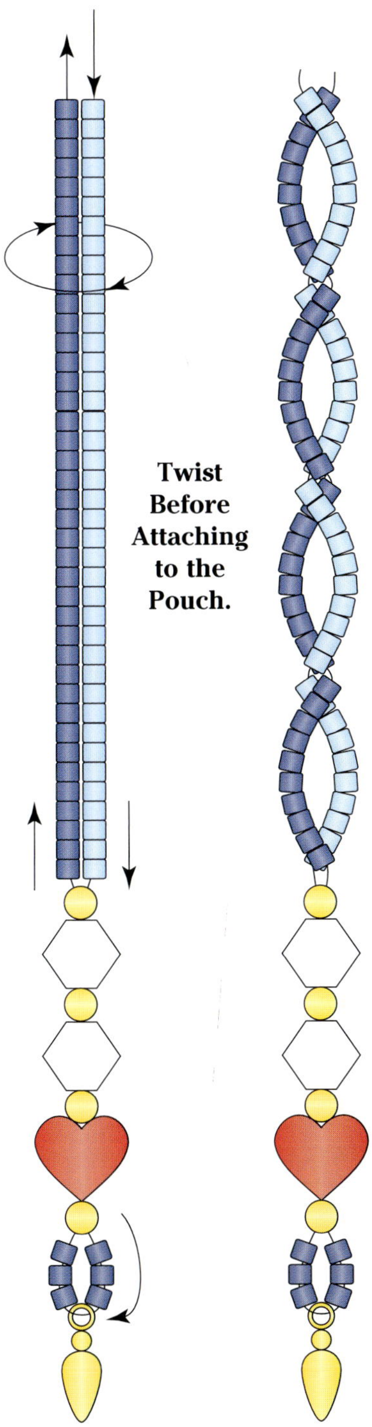

Make 17 Fringe Dangles

Angel of True Love

STITCHES:
- Tubular Peyote on page 5
- Flat Peyote - Odd Count on page 4
- Bottom Fringe
- Stringing

SIZE: 22" long

MATERIALS:

Beading supplies:
needle, size B Nymo thread

Delica Beads:
- 204 Cream Iris, flesh, arm & leg
- 208 Tan Iris, body & leg
- 653 Brown, hair
- 295 Red Iris, heart
- 031 Metallic Gold, outer heart frame
- 101 Honey, inner heart frame
- 202 White AB, cloud
- 041 Clear Silver Lined, cloud outline & strap edging
- 243 Blue Iris, background
- 361 Matte Royal Blue, background

Assorted beads:
- 6 mm Red glass hearts
- 4 mm Clear Crystal bicone
- 2 mm Red Crystal bicone
- 10 mm Gold drop charm

15 mm Gold key charm

INSTRUCTIONS:

Pouch Body:
Weave the body of the pouch in Tubular Peyote.

Paper Tube:
TIP: It is easier to stitch Tubular Peyote around a form. Often you can find a cardboard tube or even a small bottle the correct size to fit inside of the pouch as you stitch.

If you cannot find a cardboard tube the right size, make one from rolled paper, see page 30.

Bottom of Pouch:
Remove the cardboard tube. Weave the flap at the bottom of the pouch.

Close Pouch:
Close the bottom of the pouch by stitching beads together.

Weave the clouds in Flat Peyote - Odd Count (on page 4), and add to the bottom of purse as shown.

Fringe:
Add Twisted Fringe to the bottom of pouch, in between the clouds. Add 2 beads of each shade of Blue to make graduated lengths toward the center.

Necklace Strap:
Weave the neck strap in Flat Peyote - Odd Count, embellished with words and with clouds.

You can weave your own message into the strap, or leave it plain.

Weave the strap first, add the ends of each cloud.

Add a Silver Picot stitch edge.

Attach to purse on each side as shown.

Add Blue and Silver Branch Fringe. Refer to page 23 for Branch Fringe diagram, but make each of these longer.

Tribal Doll

STITCHES:
- Tubular Peyote
- Flat Peyote - Odd Count
- Ladder Stitch
- Bottom Fringe
- Stringing

SIZE: 5" long

MATERIALS:

Delica beads:
- 010 Black hex, body
- 651 Pale Orange, vest
- 608 Silver Lined Teal, vest

Assorted Colorful beads
- 2 disc beads for neck
- 4 Black glass donuts - 6 mm
- 2 Red glass drop beads- 8 mm
- 2 Hand charms

Assorted charms and bells
1¼" Head bead
Pin back

Beading supplies:
- needle
- size B Nymo thread

INSTRUCTIONS:

Arms and Legs:
Begin by weaving 2 arms and 2 legs in Tubular Peyote. Bead around a straw or chopstick to support the tubes. Add points at the top of arms. Fold flat with points aligned, and add Ladder stitch bead loops with glass donuts as shown in diagram.
Sew in charms or beads for hands and feet.

Body:
Following chart, weave in Tubular Peyote. Remove straw. Weave the flaps at the bottom. When completed, fold flat with points aligned. Attach legs with Ladder stitch bead loop.

Vest:
Following chart, weave from center line to bottom edge in Flat Peyote - Odd Count.
Repeat for other side.
See diagram for place to attach arms under shoulder flaps with bead loops.

Assembly:
Secure thread to center top of body. Take thread through center of vest, neck beads, head bead and top bead. Go back through head, neck and into body to secure. Repeat several times for added strength. Glue the pin onto back of the head bead.

Embellishment:
Make a necklace for the doll, sewing ends to the front of vest. Sew belt and dangles to sides of vest.

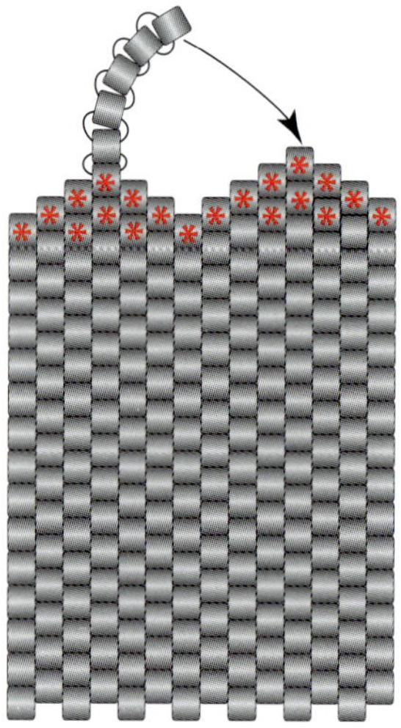

Arms - Make 2

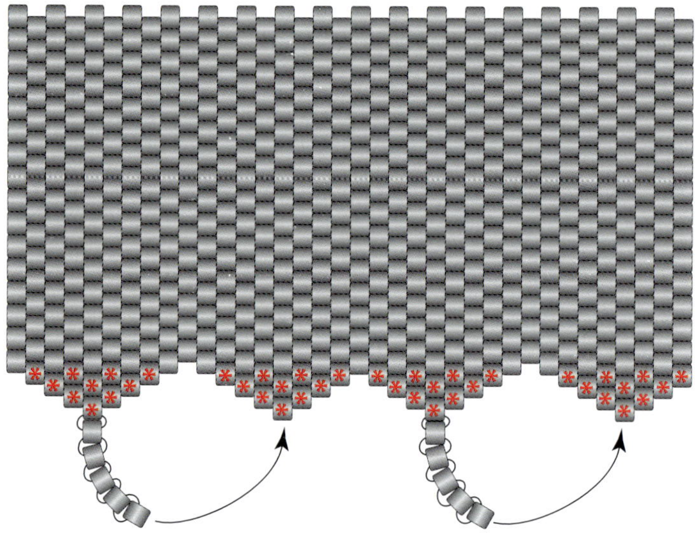

Body - Make 1

* Flaps

Legs - Make 2

* Arm Placement

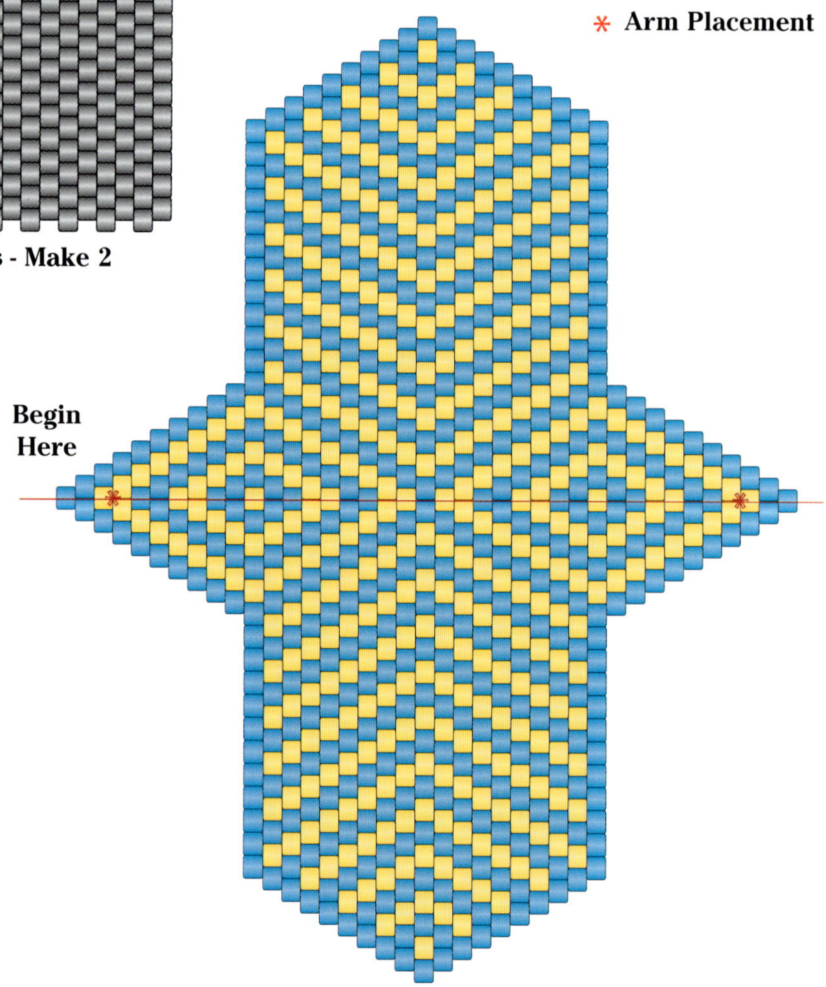

Vest - Make 1

Tribal Doll

From the top of his head to the tips of his toes, this tribal doll is wonderful.

Check out the bright vest, neck jewelry and belt with fringe ending in bells.

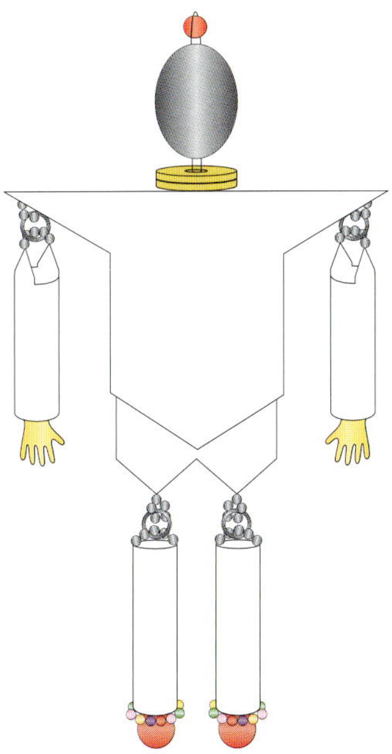

Attach legs and arms with Ladder Stitch bead loops and donuts.

Attach Legs to Body

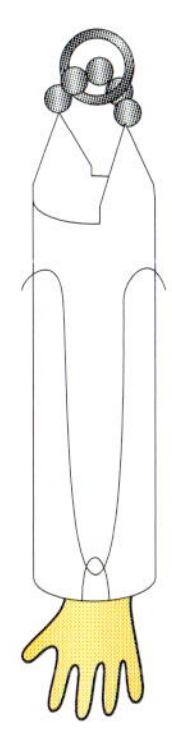

Attach Hands to Arms

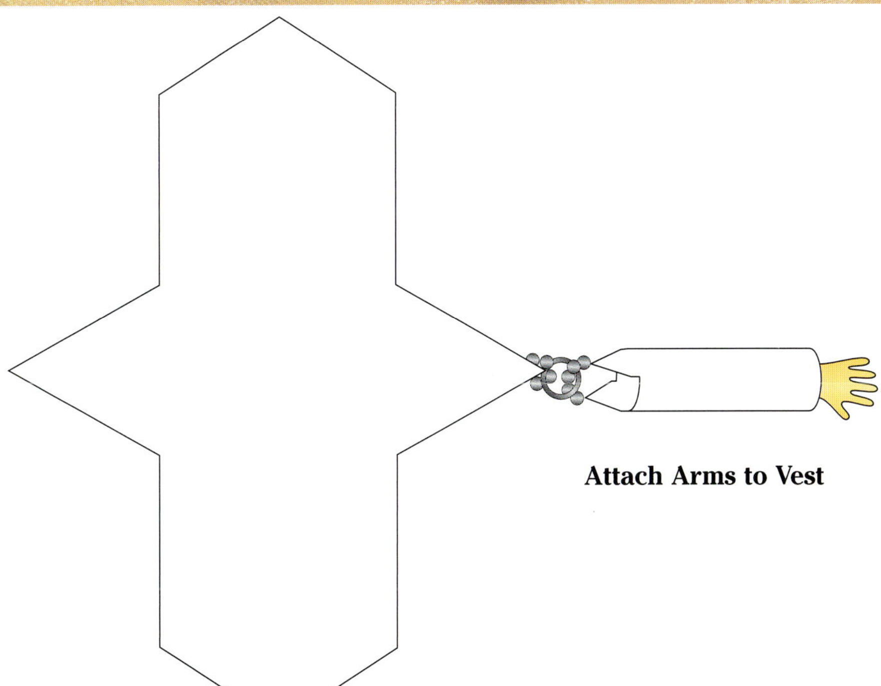

Attach Arms to Vest

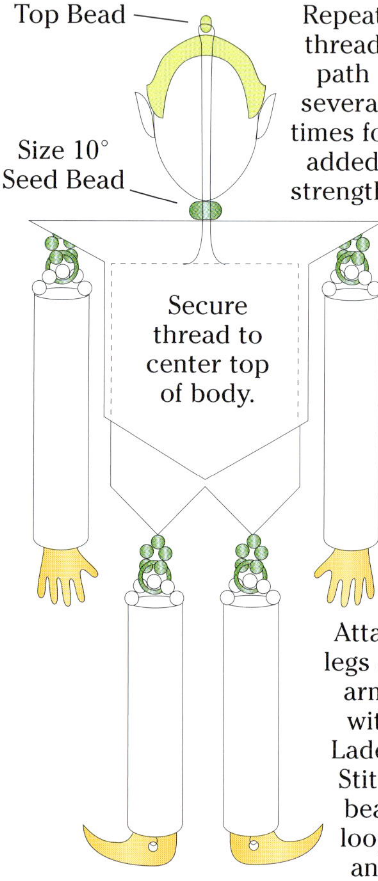

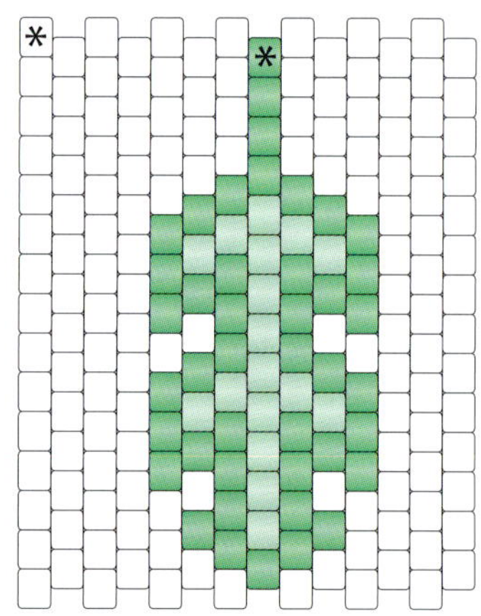

Arms - Make 2

Legs - Make 2

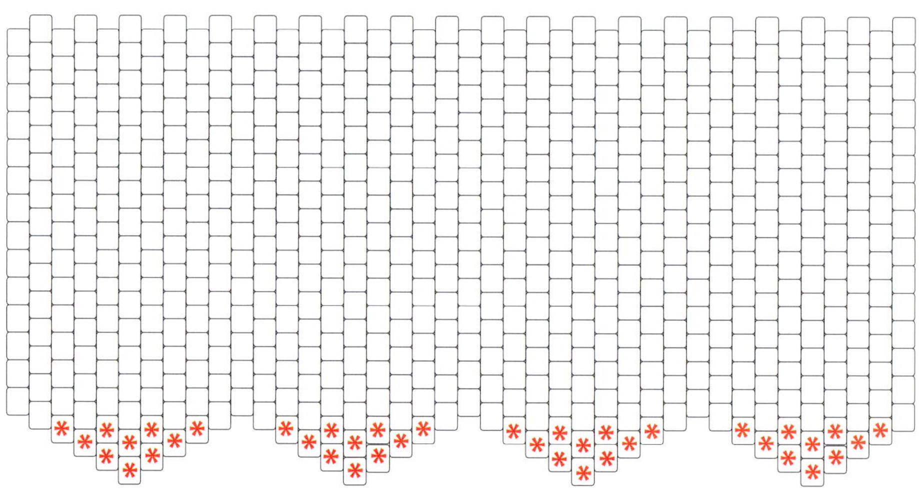

Body - Make 1

Pixie Doll

This little woodland sprite is delightful. Exquisitely detailed, this fanciful being makes itself at home as a fashion pin or ornament.

A leaf vest covers his torso and around his neck he carries a lei made of flowers, leaves and ladybugs.

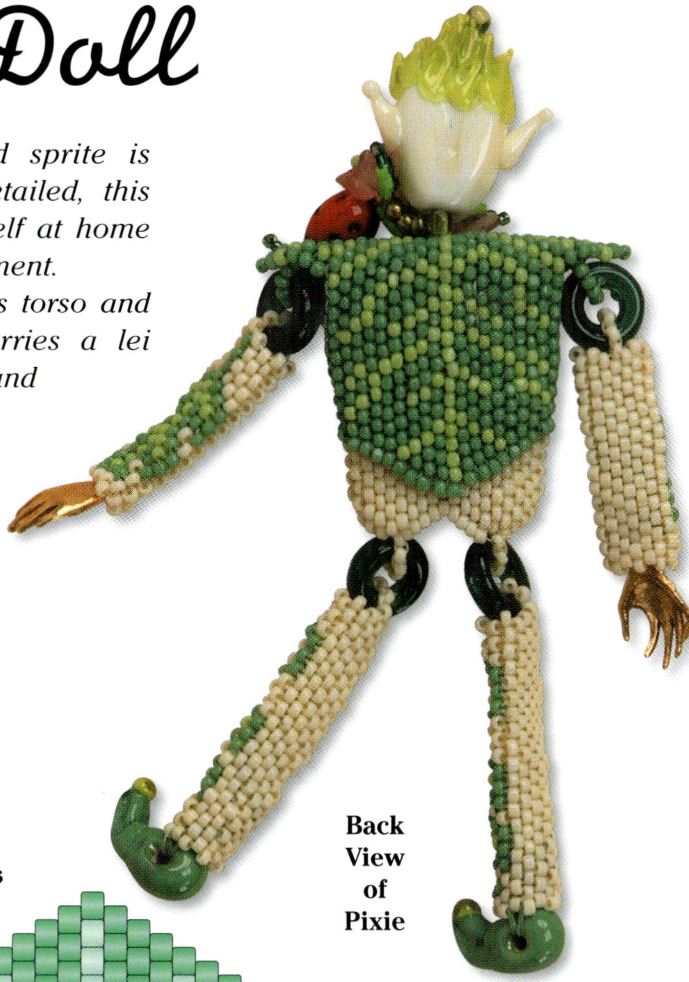

Back View of Pixie

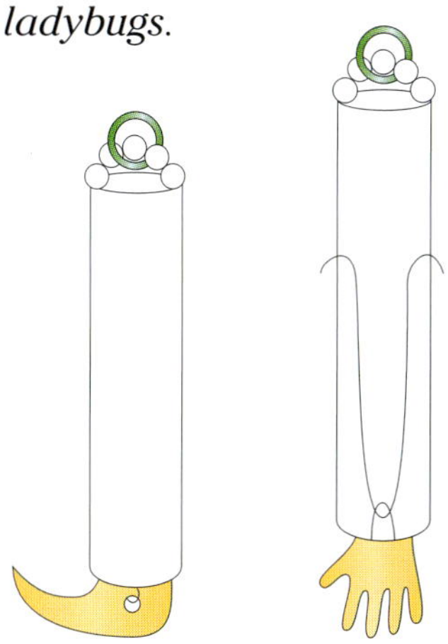

Attach Feet to Legs **Attach Hands to Arms**

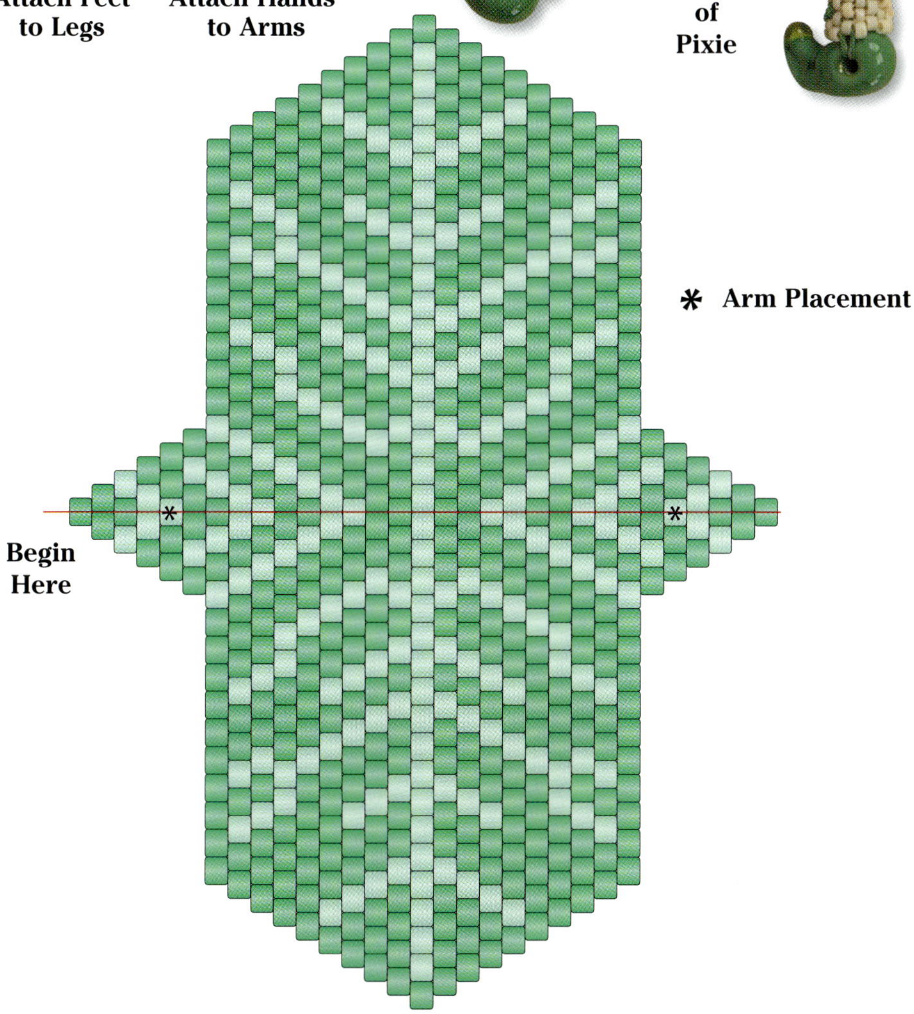

Vest - Make 1

Pixie Doll

beaded by Shirleen Fennema

STITCHES:
- Tubular Peyote
- Flat Peyote - Odd Count
- Ladder Stitch
- Stringing

SIZE: 3¾" long

MATERIALS:

Delica:
- 203 Cream Iris, body
- 274 Grass Green Iris, vest & motif
- 724 Leaf Green, vest & motif

Assorted beads:
- 4 Green 8 mm glass donuts
- 2 Ladybug beads
- Leaf bead
- 1 Green size 10° seed bead
- 1 Head bead
- 2 Feet beads
- 2 Brass hand charms
- ½" pin back

Beading supplies:
- needle
- size B Nymo thread

INSTRUCTIONS:

Arms and Legs:
Begin by weaving 2 arms and 2 legs in Tubular Peyote. Bead around a straw or chopstick to support the tubes. Fold arms and legs flat with pattern to the front and add Ladder Stitch bead loops with glass donuts as shown in diagram.

Sew in charms or beads for hands and feet.

Body:
Weave in Tubular Peyote. Remove straw. Weave the flaps at the bottom. When completed, fold flat with points aligned. Attach legs with Ladder stitch bead loops.

Vest:
Following chart, weave in Flat Peyote - Odd-Count from the center line to the bottom edge. Repeat for other side.

Attach arms to vest.

Place the cape over the neck before attaching head. Tack vest to body just below neck on the front and back.

Assembly:
Secure thread to the center top of body. Take thread through the center of vest, through the size 10° Green seed bead, head bead and top bead. Go back through head, neck and into body to secure. Repeat several times for added strength.

Embellishment:
Make necklace, sewing it to the front of vest.

Sew pin back in place.

Tiny Goddess

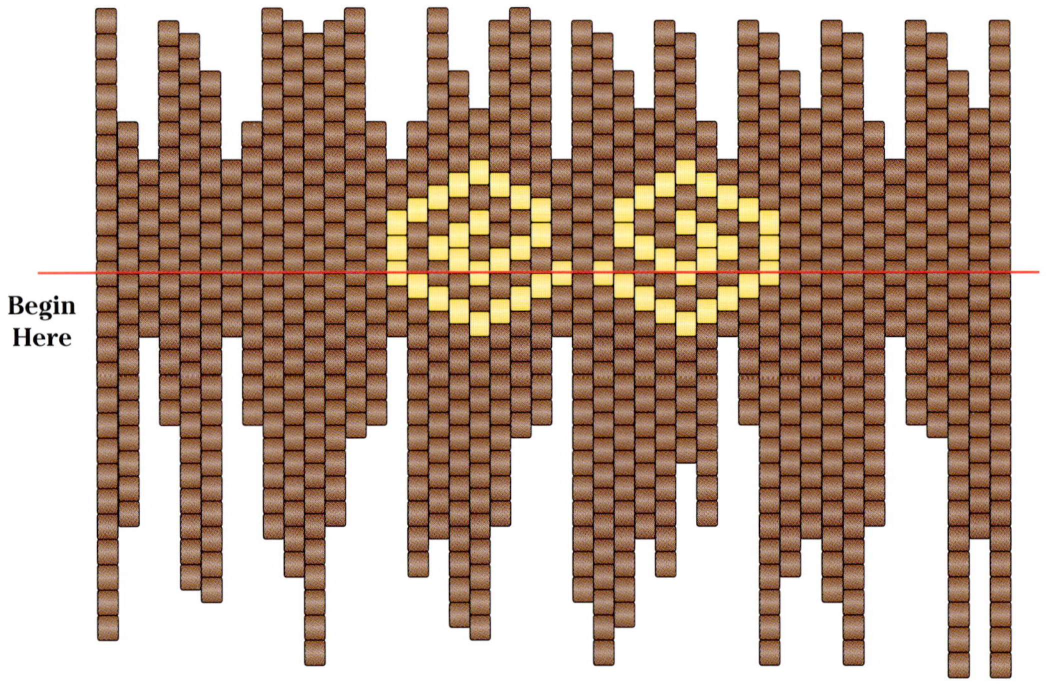

Body Beading Pattern

Omit Bead

Skip these beads for decrease, add them back for increase.

Goddesses from ancient times had powers to make one's deepest wishes come true. Often people would hold a goddess totem in their hand while meditating.

A goddess is a symbol of the ancient power that we all have within us, the power to make our deepest wishes come true.

☐ **Omit Bead**

Skip these beads for decrease, add them back for increase.

Begin Here

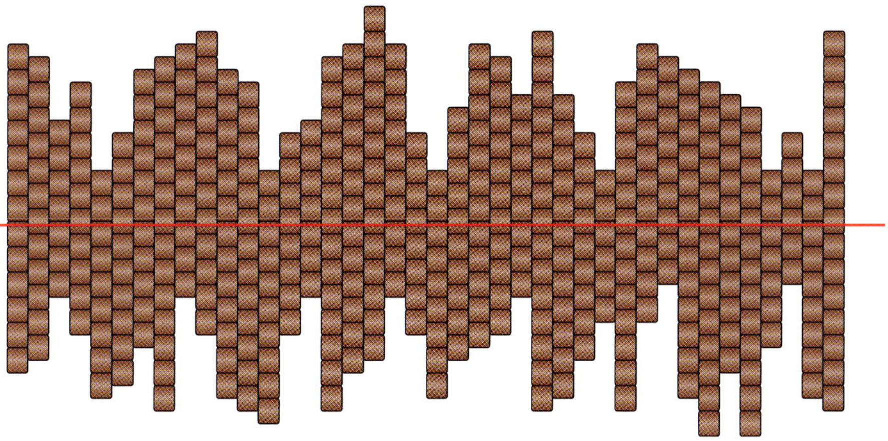

Head Beading Pattern

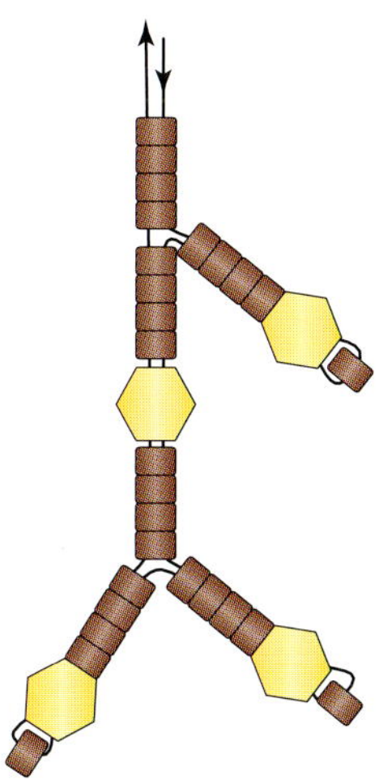

Branch Fringe

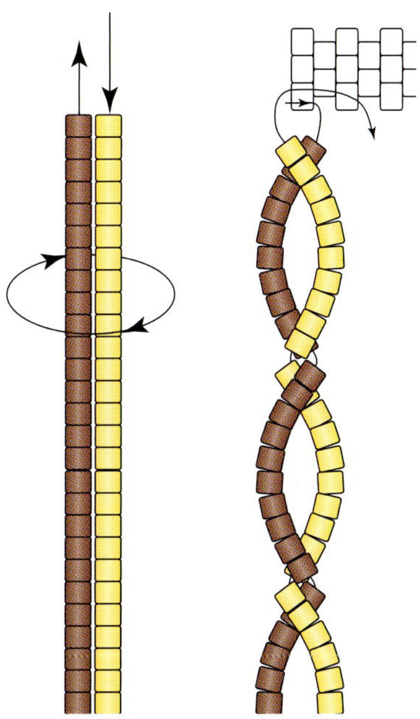

Twisted Fringe

Tiny Goddesses

beaded by
Sharon Berschemer

STITCHES:
- Tubular Peyote
- Branch Fringe
- Twisted Fringe
- Stringing

SIZE: 2½" long

BASIC MATERIALS:
⅝" wooden bead
Beading supplies:
- needle
- size B Nymo thread)

BASIC INSTRUCTIONS:

Body:
Weave in Tubular Peyote beginning at the "Begin Here" line. Work down to the bottom. Stuff the body firmly at this point with poly fiberfill.

Go back to "Begin Here" line and work up to the neck.

Head:
Weave around the wooden bead in Tubular Peyote following the chart. Sew to neck of body.

Brown Goddess

Delica beads:
- 031 Metallic Gold, motif
- 653 Brown, body
- 203 Cream Iris, necklace
- 010 Black hex, hair

Embellishments:
Add Branch Fringe for hair.
Add a necklace of cream beads.

Black Goddess

MATERIALS:
Delica beads:
- 031 Metallic Gold, motif
- 010 Black hex, body & fringe

Brass charms

INSTRUCTIONS:

Embellishments:
Add charm earrings to the head.
Add twisted fringe at the bottom.

White Goddess

MATERIALS:
Delica beads:
- 22L Metallic Bronze, motif
- 203 Cream Iris, body

10 mm Bronze drop beads
Brass charms

INSTRUCTIONS:

Embellishments:
Make a necklace using Bronze seed beads and charms.

Chiapas Tassel

This Chiapas woman is beautifully dressed. Her bright hat and jacket are adorned with a parrot, flowers and leaves on a beaded vine.

A spectacular show of color, this wonderful Chiapas Doll is a fabulous way to enjoy the art of beading. Designed as a tribute to the women of the Chiapas Indians in Mexico, this project is best suited to the experienced beader.

continued on pages 39 - 40

Chiapas Tassel

STITCHES:
- Tubular Peyote
- Flat Peyote - Odd Count
- Bottom Fringe
- Ladder Stitch
- Stringing

SIZE: 8" long

MATERIALS:

5/8" wood bead

Delica beads:
- 010 Black, braids, skirt motif
- 610 Silver Lined Deep Purple, motif
- 253 Lavender Iris, motif
- 721 Opaque Yellow, motif
- 653 Brown, head
- 161 Orange AB, motif
- 608 Silver Lined Teal, motif
- 124 Celery AB, motif
- 201 White Iris, body
- 295 Red Iris, jacket hat, arms

Assorted beads:
- 2 Red 8 mm glass donuts
- 13 Green 10 mm glass leaves
- 14 Red 10 mm glass flowers beads
- Green faceted tube beads
- Light Green seed, Yellow iridescent seed, Orange flat ovals

Assorted fibers for tassel

Small painted bird

Assorted charms

Beading supplies:
needle, size B Nymo thread

INSTRUCTIONS:

Body:

Weave body in Tubular Peyote following chart on page 38. The blank sections on the chart show decreases and increases which shape the body. Stuff top of body with fiberfill stuffing to help it hold its shape.

Add skirt fringe to the bottom.

INSTRUCTIONS:

Head:

Cover a wooden bead following chart on page 40. Add braids in twisted fringe. Add earrings. Attach head to neck of body. Sew around head and neck again for added strength.

Arms:

Weave arms in Tubular Peyote following chart on page 40. Attach glass donuts at the top with a Ladder stitch loop.

Sew in hand charms.

Jacket:

Weave in Flat Peyote - Odd-Count from the 'Begin Here' line to the bottom edge of the chart on page 40. Repeat for the other side.

Embellish with Light Green seed beads, Red flower beads and Green leaves.

Attach each arm as indicated on chart with a Ladder stitch loop.

Attach jacket to doll, tacking securely to the front and back.

Necklace:

Bring thread out of the back of neck. String half of the necklace, attach to front of doll. String the second half and go around again for added strength.

Tassel:

Make tassel following diagrams.

Insert the wrapped end into the bottom of the beaded skirt. Tack to skirt in about a dozen places, sewing back and forth. Cut looped ends of yarn evenly at bottom of tassel.

Hat:

Make hat following chart on page 38.

Attach bird charm and loop for hanging.

Chiapas Tassel

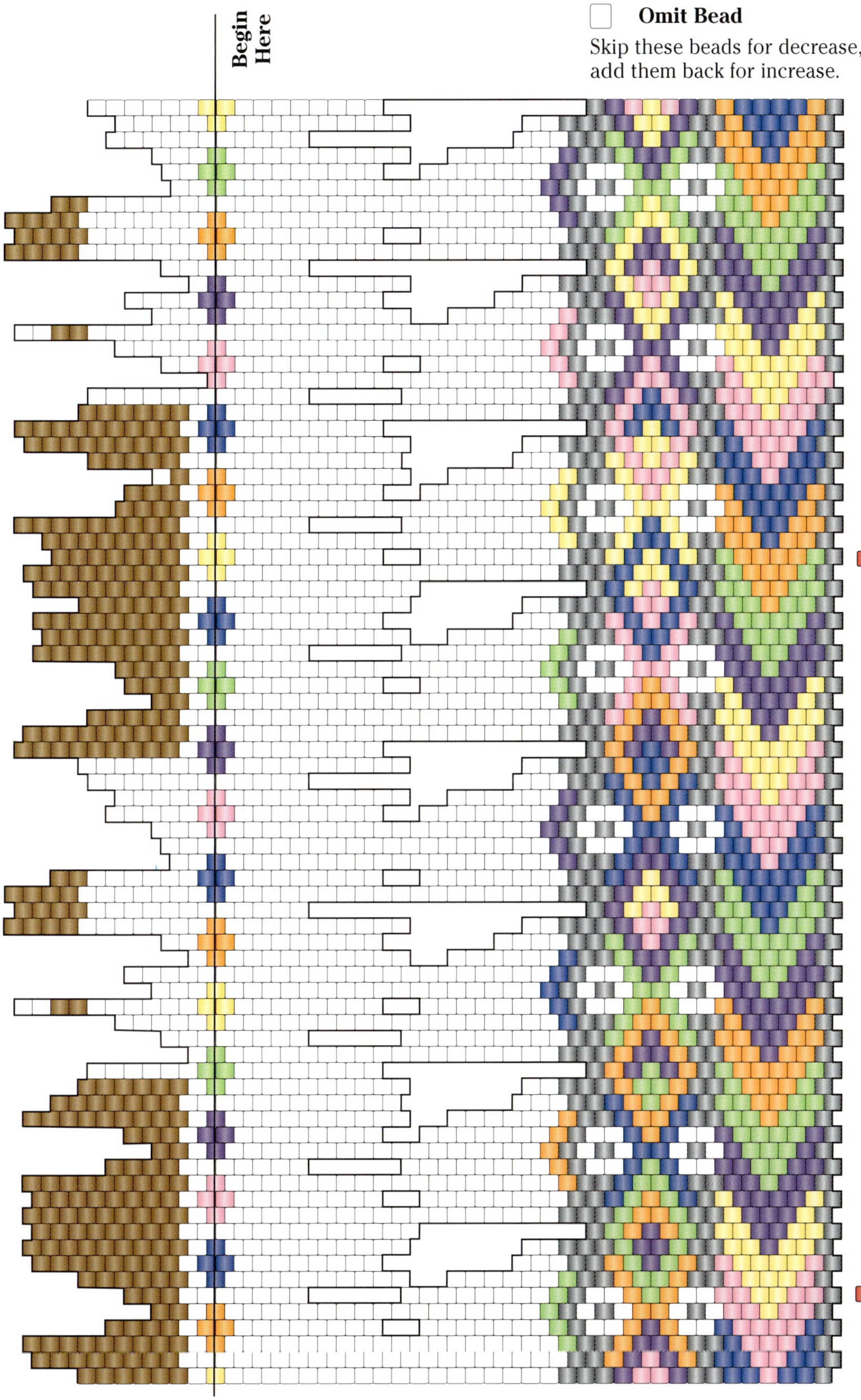

Dress Beading Pattern

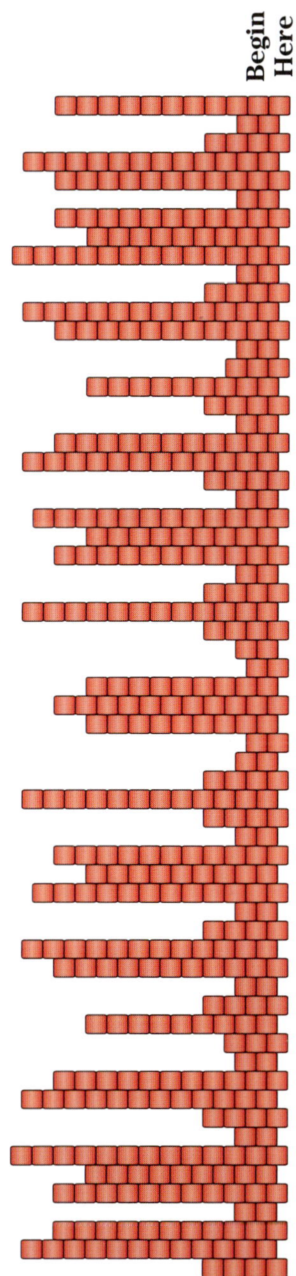

Hat Pattern

continued from pages 38 - 39

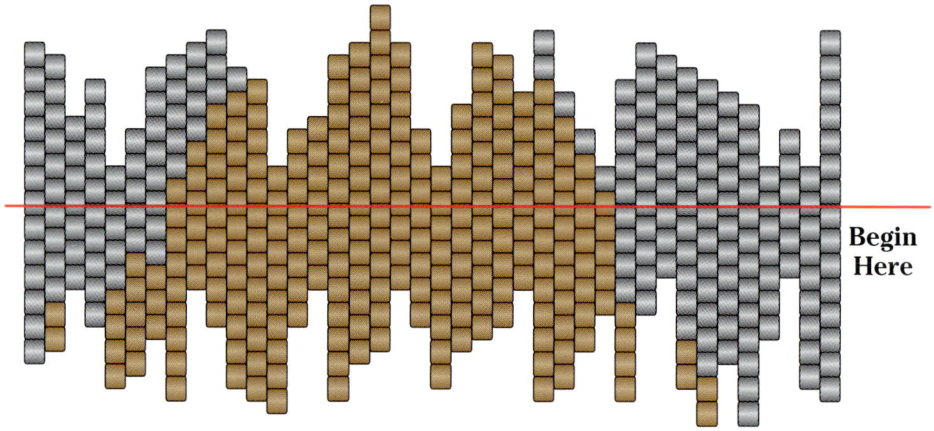

Head Beading Pattern

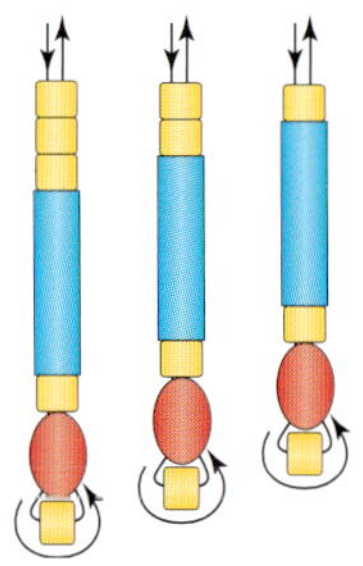

Fringe Pattern

Arms Pattern - Make 2

*** Attach Arms**

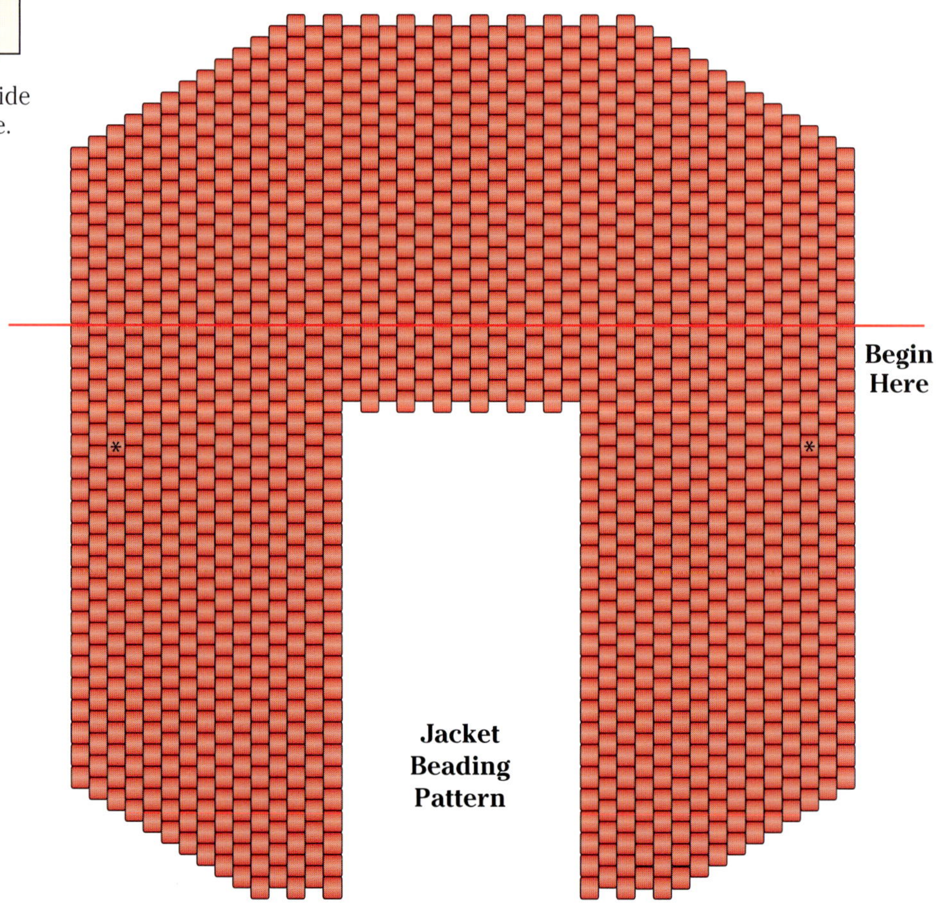

Jacket Beading Pattern

Tassel Diagrams

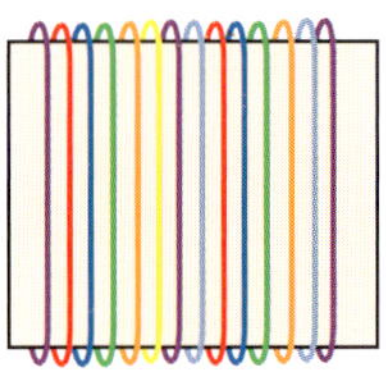

1. Wrap assorted fibers around cardboard.

2. Gather one side together and tie.

3. Wrap enough yarn around the top of tassel to fit snugly under skirt.

4. Cut looped ends of yarn evenly at the bottom of tassel.

Pixie Tassel

This Pixie is the tassel of tassels!

She is full of forest motifs and covered with leaves. She even has small leaf beads on her head. White flower beads decorate the bodice; fibers and ribbons form the skirt.

continued on pages 42 - 43

 **Omit Bead**

Skip these beads for decrease, add them back for increase.

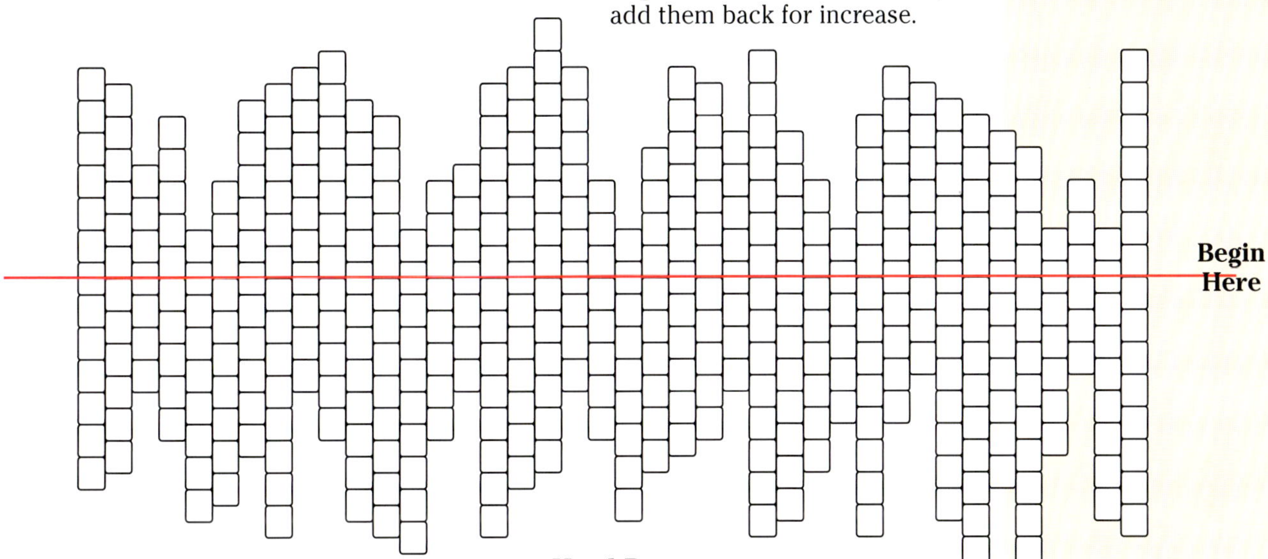

Head Pattern

*** Attach Arm**

Fold over the shoulder leaf a little before attaching it to give a bit of lift.

Shoulder Pattern - Make 2

Pixie Tassel

STITCHES:
- Tubular Peyote
- Flat Peyote - Odd Count
- Bottom Fringe
- Ladder Stitch
- Stringing

SIZE: 7½" long

MATERIALS:
⅝" wood bead

Delica beads:
- 201 White Iris, body
- 031 Metallic Gold, motif
- 373 Matte Teal Green, motif

Assorted beads:
- 14 mm Pale Green AB leaf beads
- 8 mm Frosted AB leaf beads
- 8 mm Clear glass donuts
- 10 mm Milk glass flower beads
- 5 mm Frosted glass disc beads

Beading supplies:
- needle, size B Nymo thread

Assorted fibers for tassel

continued from pages 41

Arm Pattern - Make 2

Tassel Diagrams

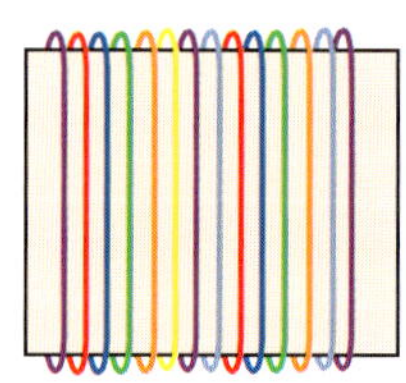

1. Wrap assorted fibers around cardboard.

2. Gather one side together and tie.

3. Wrap enough yarn around the top of tassel to fit snugly under skirt.

4. Cut looped ends of yarn evenly at the bottom of tassel.

Pixie Tassel

INSTRUCTIONS:

Body:

Weave body in Tubular Peyote following the chart on page 41.

Attach Flower beads on the top where indicated.

Stuff the top of body with poly fiberfill to help hold its shape.

Head:

Cover a wooden bead following the chart on page 42.

Add leaf beads for a headdress.

Attach the head to neck of body. Sew around again for added strength.

Arms:

Weave arms in Tubular Peyote following chart on page 43. Flatten arms with the pattern on the front, with points aligned.

Attach glass donuts to points with a Ladder Stitch loop.

Sew in leaf beads for hands.

Leaf Shoulders:

Weave shoulders in Flat Peyote - Odd Count following the chart on page 42.

Attach arms where indicated. Attach to body.

Tassel:

Make a tassel following diagrams.

Insert the wrapped end into the bottom of the beaded skirt.

Tack to skirt securely to the bottom of beaded skirt.

Cut looped ends of fibers evenly at bottom of tassel.

Pixie Tassel

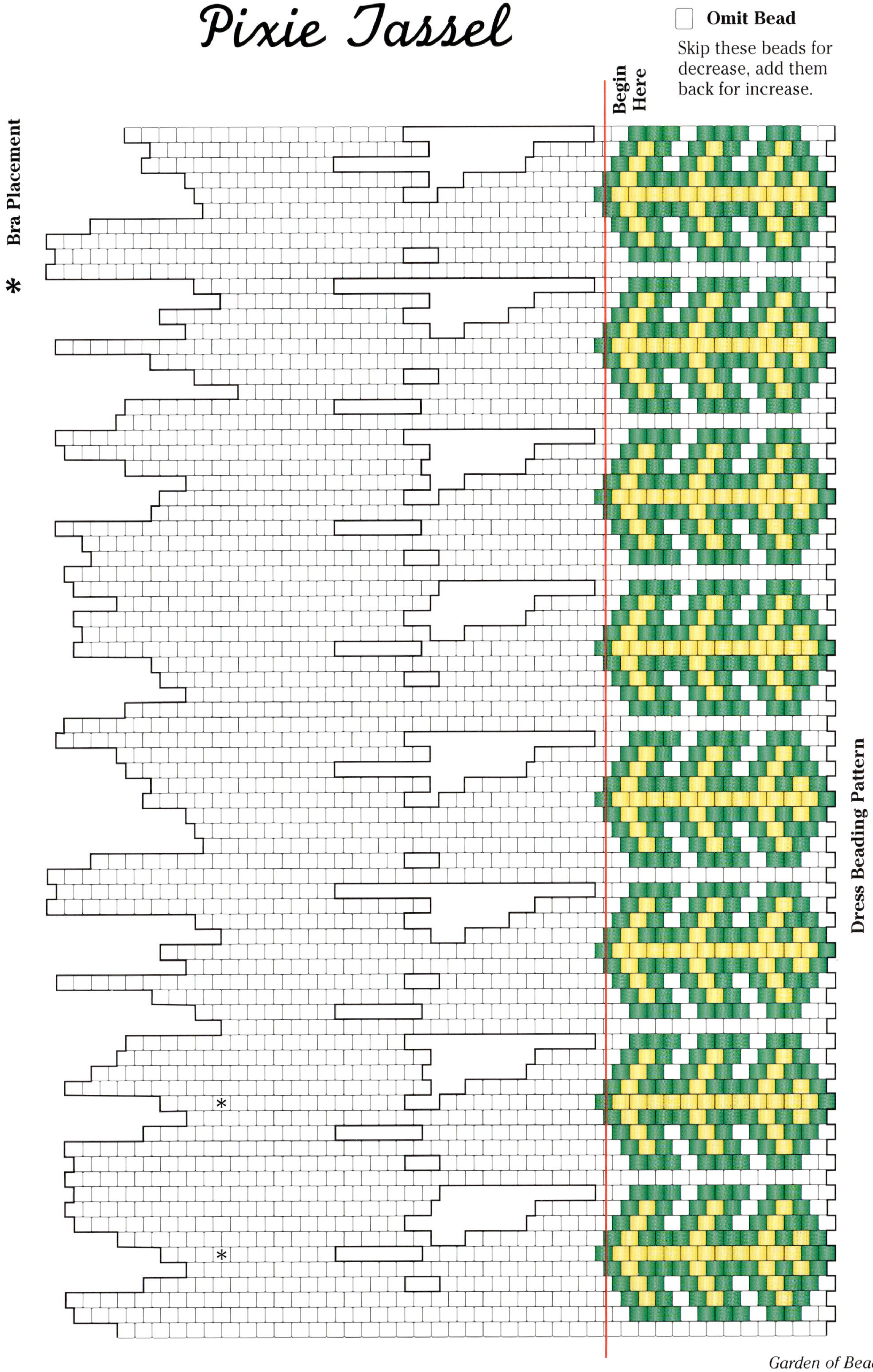

Asante Princess Tassel

This princess represents royalty at its finest!

The design was inspired by an article in National Geographic Magazine. The Asante tribe is one of the wealthiest on the African continent. To make this unique doll, follow the the colorful beading patterns for her body, arms and cape.

continued on pages 46 - 47

Asante Princess

STITCHES:
- Tubular Peyote
- Flat Peyote - Odd Count
- Bottom Fringe
- Ladder Stitch
- Stringing

SIZE: 8" long

MATERIALS:

5/8" wood bead

Delica beads:
- 410 Metallic Gold, cape, arms, skirt motif
- 653 Brown, body
- 682 Silver Lined Orange, motif
- 011 Metallic Olive Green, motif

Assorted beads:
- 3 mm Brass spacer beads
- 5 mm saturn beads - Green & Gold
- 6 mm Amber rice beads
- 8 mm Tortoise glass donuts
- Assorted Brass charms
- 2 Brass hand charms

Assorted fibers for tassel

Assorted feathers - Red, Green, Black

Beading supplies:
needle, size B Nymo thread

INSTRUCTIONS:

Body:
Weave body in Tubular Peyote following the chart on page 44. The blank sections on the chart show decreases and increases which shape the body.

Stuff the top of the body with poly fiberfill to help it hold its shape.

Add coin charms to points on the skirt with Ladder Stitch bands.

Cape:
Weave in Flat Peyote - Odd Count from 'Begin Here' at the center line to the bottom edge.

Repeat for the top edge.

Add coin charms to points on the cape with Ladder Stitch bands.

Arms:
Weave arms in Tubular Peyote following the chart on page 45.

Flatten arms with the pattern on front, with points aligned. Attach donuts to the arms at the points with Ladder Stitch loop.

Sew in hand charms. Attach arms to the cape as indicated on chart on page 45.

Head:
Cover a wooden bead following the chart on page 46.

Drape the cape over the neck.

Attach the head to the neck of body. Sew around again for added strength.

Tassel:
Make a tassel following the diagrams.

Insert the wrapped end into the bottom of the beaded skirt. Tack to skirt in about a dozen places, sewing back and forth.

Cut looped ends of fibers at the bottom of tassel.

Embellishment:
Glue feathers into the top of bead. Add beads around feathers, tacking to back of head.

Add a necklace and earrings.

Omit Bead

Skip these beads for decrease, add them back for increase.

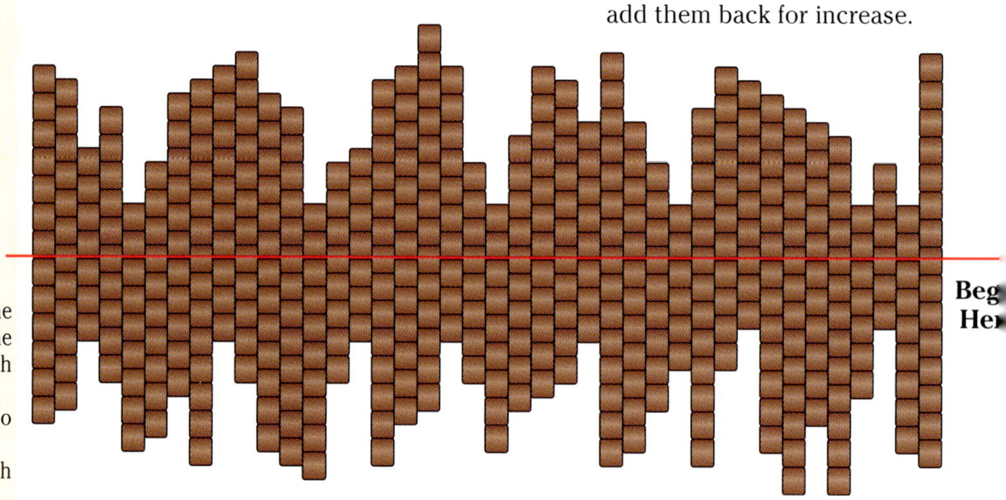

Asante Princess Head Pattern - Make 1

Tassel Diagrams

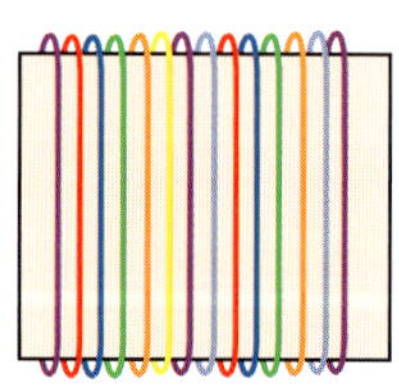

1. Wrap assorted fibers around cardboard.

2. Gather one side together and tie.

3. Wrap enough yarn around the top of tassel to fit snugly under skirt.

4. Cut looped ends of yarn evenly at the bottom of tassel.

Color Conversion Chart
for Cylinder Beads

Delica	Toho	Color
01	81	Shiny Pewter
10	49	Black
11	83	Metallic Olive Green
22	221A	Metallic Mahogany
22L	221	Metallic Bronze
24	508	Green Amber
27	506	Green Topaz
31	712	Metallic Gold
35	558	Metallic Silver
41	21	Clear Silver Lined
54	904	Apricot Lined AB
64	278	Oyster AB
67	794	Pale Peach Lined AB
73	790	Violet Lined Clear AB
74	790	Violet Lined Clear AB
79	793	Aqua Lined Clear AB
85	782	Blue AB
101	103	Honey
122	454	Sienna AB
124	457	Celery AB
125	322	Metallic Green AB
151	174	Clear Light Orange AB
152	795	Clear Lime AB
160	402	Yellow AB
161	165	Orange AB
162	405	Dark Fuchsia AB
183	28	Silver Lined Cobalt Blue
201	121	White Iris
202	401	White AB
203	122	Cream Iris
204	123	Cream Iris
208	948	Tan Iris
243	917	Blue Iris
253	166	Lavender Iris
274	795	Grass Green Iris
276	180	Metallic Dark Green
295	798	Red Iris
310	610	Matte Black
340	423F	Matte Copper
352	762	Matte Ivory
361	48F	Matte Royal Blue
371	262	Fatigue Green
373	940	Matte Teal Green
410	557	Metallic Gold
415	561	Light Green
461	501	Metallic Brown
607	27BD	Silver Lined Blue Spruce
608	27BD	Silver Lined Teal
609	28	Silver Lined Royal Purple
610	28	Silver Lined Deep Purple
651	950	Pale Orange
652	353	Gray
653	951	Brown
682	30	Silver Lined Orange
704	798	Clear Red
721	42	Opaque Yellow
723	45	Opaque Red
724	47	Leaf Green
746	7F	Matte Grass Green
747	3F	Matte Light Blue
748	8F	Matte Blue
771	2F	Matte Ecru
1333	30	Silver Lined Orange
1340	563	Silver Lined Fuchsia
1345	461	Silver Lined Dark Fuschia
1347	607	Silver Lined Purple

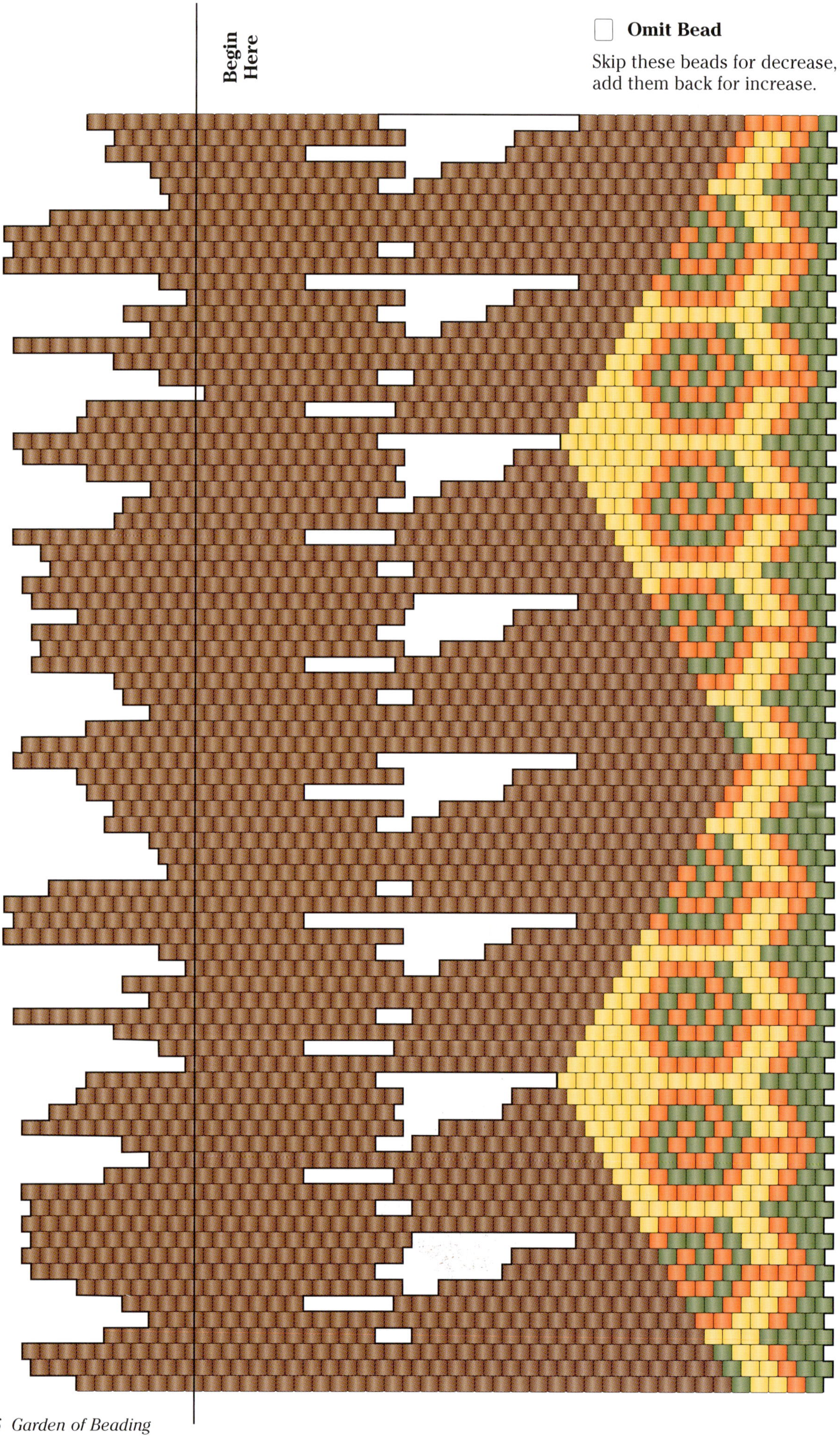

Asante Princess Body Pattern

Asante Princess Tassel

Plumes of glorious feathers become a headpiece encircled by two rows of beads. Spirit swirls decorate the collar, arms and skirt of the doll's costume.

Matching earrings and a necklace adorn the princess and gold coins dangle from beaded points. The skirt is made from a mix of colorful fibers.

continued from pages 44 - 45

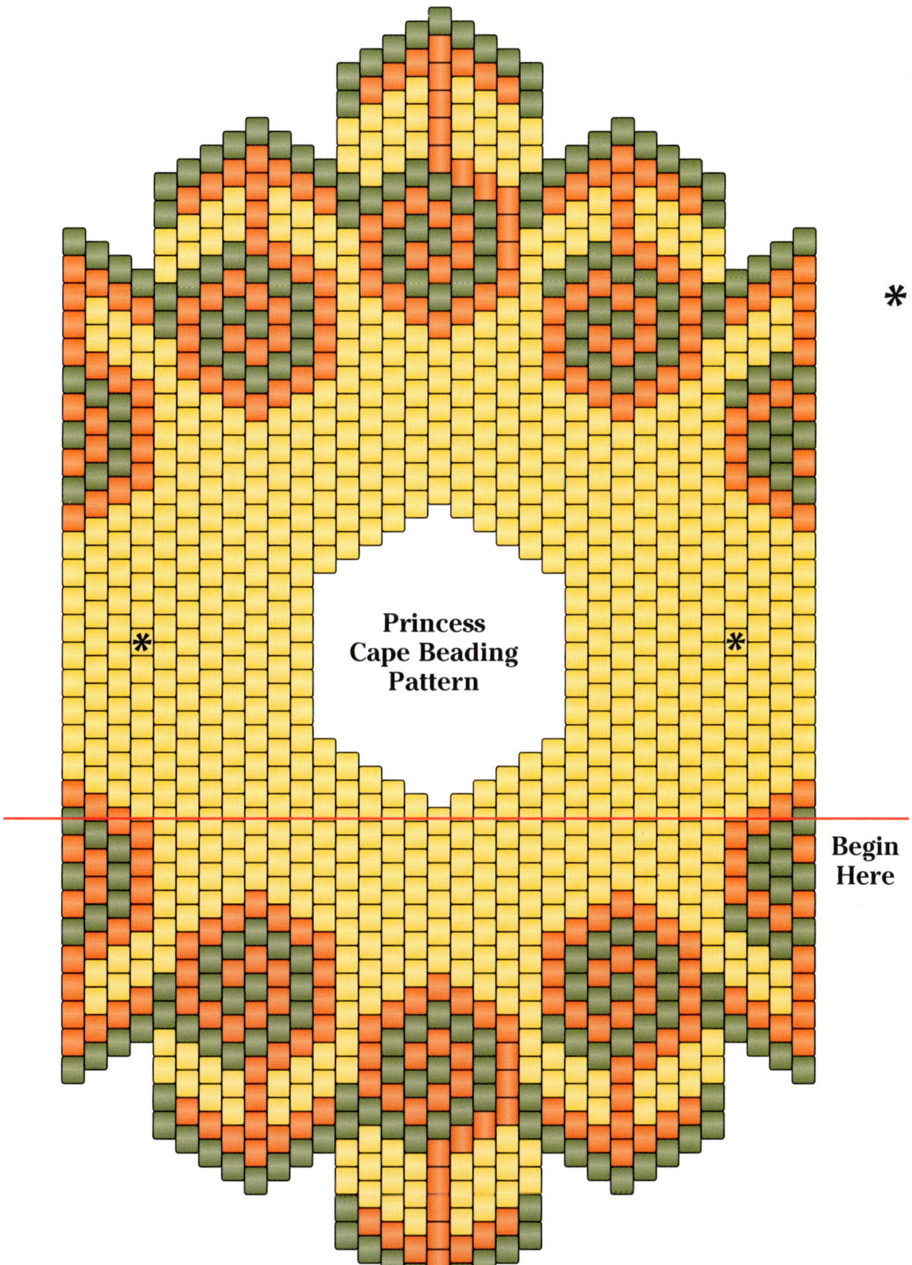

Princess Cape Beading Pattern

* Attach arms

Princess Arm Pattern - Make 2

Earth Pixie
beaded by Jill Cremer

STITCHES:
- Tubular Peyote
- Flat Peyote - Odd Count
- Bottom Fringe
- Ladder Stitch
- Stringing

SIZE: 4½" long

MATERIALS:
⅝" wood bead

Beading supplies:
needle, size B Nymo thread

Delica beads:
- 723 Opaque Red, wrist
- 340 Matte Copper, body
- 1333 Silver Lined Orange, motif for arms & legs
- 276 Metallic Dark Green, motif
- 746 Matte Grass Green, motif

Assorted beads:
- 8 mm Clear glass donuts
- Green AB leaf beads

Flower beads
- 6 mm Orange
- 6 mm Yellow
- 10 mm Red

Earth Pixie

Flowers and leaves are this pixie's costume. A flower decorates the arms and flower beads create the hands. The legs are beaded in a leaf motif and the feet are leaf beads.

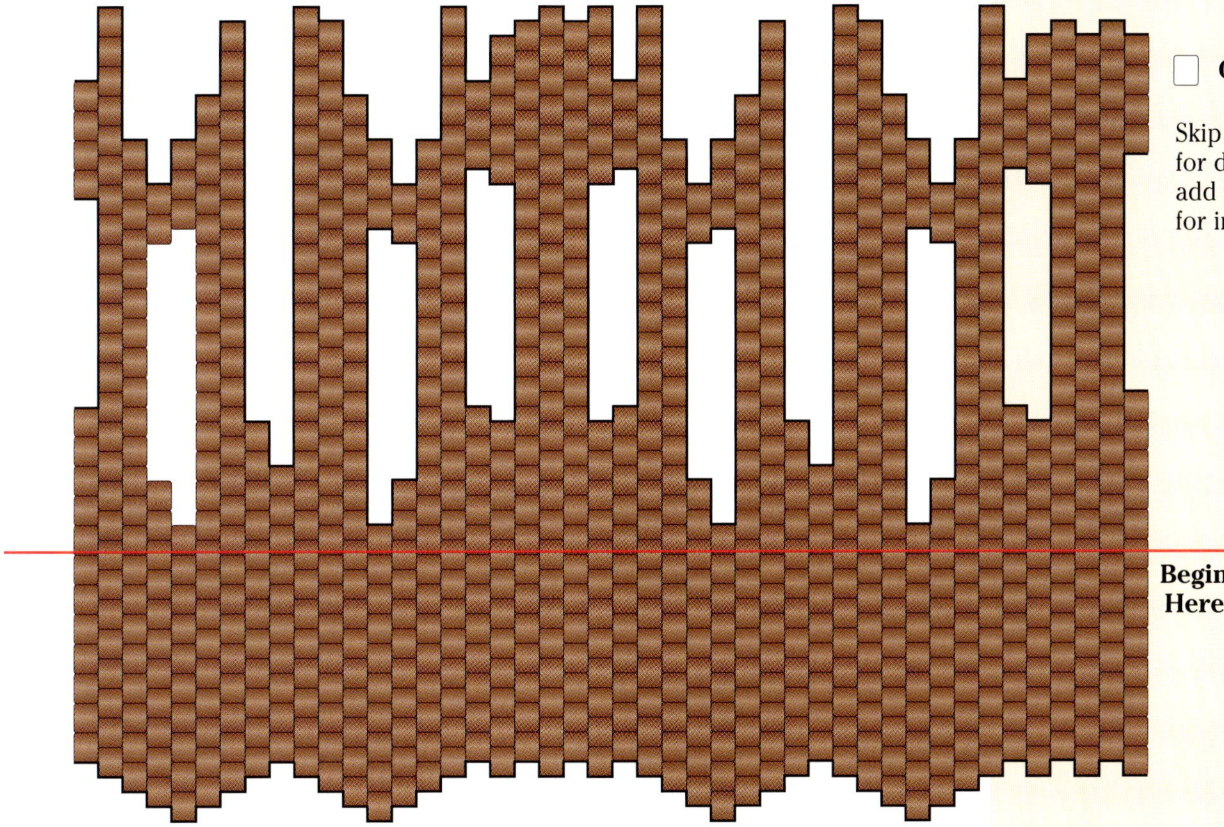

Begin Here

Omit Bead

Skip these beads for decrease, add them back for increase.

*** Attach to body**

Body Beading Pattern

Leg Pattern - Make 2

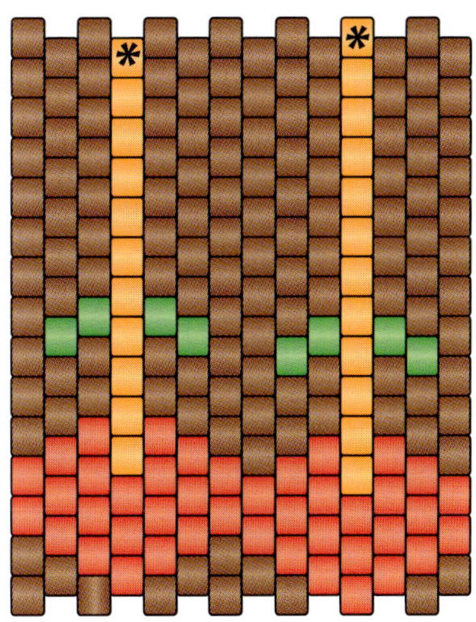

Arm Pattern - Make 2

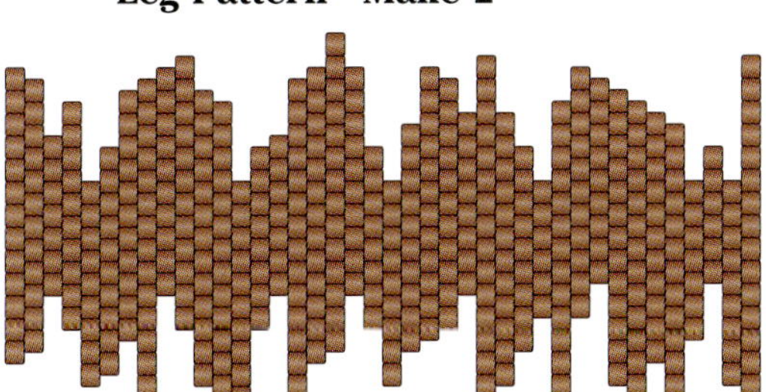

Note:: Use the larger head pattern chart on page 46. Substitute White beads for Flower Pixie.

Shoulder Pattern - Make 2

INSTRUCTIONS:

Arms and Legs:

Begin by weaving 2 arms and 2 legs in Tubular Peyote following the charts. Bead around a straw or chopstick to support the tubes.

Fold arms and legs flat with the pattern to front, with points aligned.

Add Ladder Stitch bead loops with glass donuts, similar to the diagram on page 33.

Sew in charms or beads for hands and feet.

Body:

Weave body in Tubular Peyote following the chart.

When completed, fold the bottom flat, with points aligned.

Attach legs to points with Ladder Stitch bead loops.

Head:

Cover a wooden bead following the head chart.

Add leaf and flower beads for a headdress.

Attach the head to neck of body. Sew around again for added strength.

Shoulder Leaves:

Weave shoulder pieces in Flat Peyote - Odd Count .

Attach arms.

Attach leaves to body.

Fringed Skirt:

Make a fringe skirt around the waist.

Lisa Ann Claver

Lisa has been beading for over 7 years.

She creates her own lampwork beads... goddesses, flowers, leaves and more, and loves adding them to her projects.

Lisa often draws inspiration for her designs from National Geographic magazine, and from her son Jeremiah, who is always providing new found objects and ideas for her consideration.

Lisa loves beading, and designs fabulous original figures. She has enjoyed many hours of beading with her loyal beading buddy Norah Plank. Contact Lisa at - www.lisaannclaver.com.

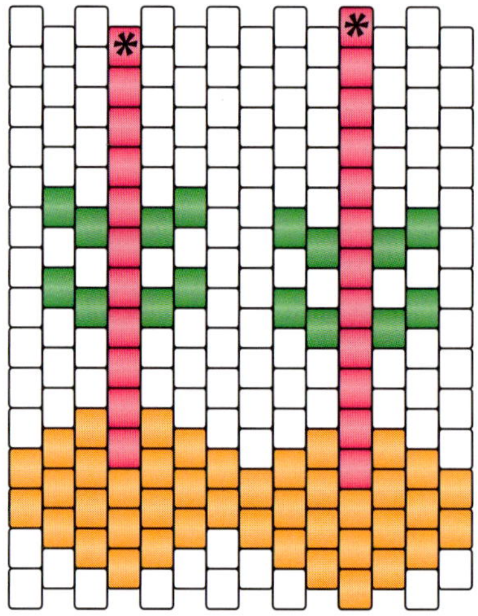

Arm Pattern - Make 2

Leg Pattern - Make 2

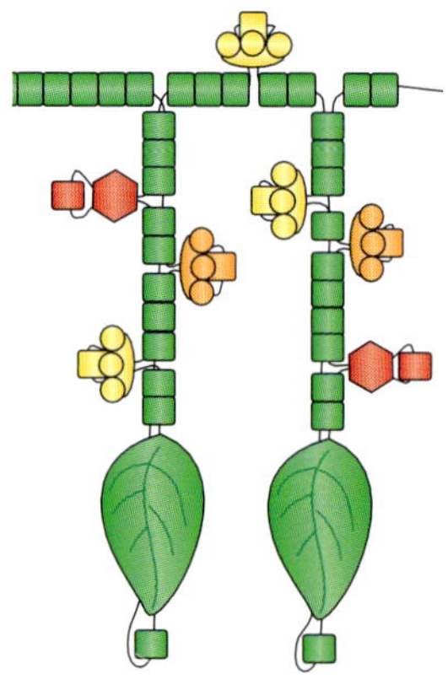

Fringe for Skirt

*** Attach Ladder Stitch Loops**

Floral Pixie

STITCHES:
- Tubular Peyote
- Flat Peyote - Odd Count
- Bottom Fringe
- Ladder Stitch
- Stringing

SIZE: 4½" long

MATERIALS:
5/8" wood bead

Delica beads:
- 161 Orange AB, motif
- 1340 Silver Lined Fuchsia, motif
- 352 Matte Ivory, body
- 276 Metallic Dark Green, motif
- 152 Clear Lime AB, motif

Assorted beads:
- 9 mm Red Flower
- 9mm Pink Flower
- 9mm Orange Flower
- 8 mm Clear glass donuts
- 10 mm Green AB leaf
- Yellow Iridescent seed

Beading supplies:
- needle
- size B Nymo thread

INSTRUCTIONS:

Arms and Legs:
Begin by weaving 2 arms and 2 legs in Tubular Peyote following the charts. Bead around a straw or chopstick to support the tubes.

Fold arms and legs flat with the pattern to front, with points aligned.

Add Ladder Stitch bead loops with glass donuts, similar to the diagram on page 33.

Sew in charms or beads for hands and feet.

Body:
Weave body in Tubular Peyote following the chart.

When completed, fold the bottom flat, with points aligned.

Attach legs to points with Ladder Stitch bead loops.

Head:
Cover a wooden bead following the head chart.

Add leaf and flower beads for a headdress.

Attach the head to neck of body. Sew around again for added strength.

Shoulder Leaves:
Weave shoulder pieces in Flat Peyote - Odd Count.

Attach arms.

Attach leaves to body.

Fringed Skirt:
Make a fringe skirt around the waist.

Note: Use the larger body pattern chart on page 50 and head pattern chart on page 46. Substitute White beads.